Joan of Arc

Personal Recollections of Joan of Arc
Annotated

(The Historical Heroine of France During the French Revolution)

Hector Harter

Published By **Regina Loviusher**

Hector Harter

All Rights Reserved

Joan of Arc: Personal Recollections of Joan of Arc Annotated (The Historical Heroine of France During the French Revolution)

ISBN 978-1-77485-582-9

No part of this guidebook shall be reproduced in any form without permission in writing from the publisher except in the case of brief quotations embodied in critical articles or reviews.

Legal & Disclaimer

The information contained in this ebook is not designed to replace or take the place of any form of medicine or professional medical advice. The information in this ebook has been provided for educational & entertainment purposes only.

The information contained in this book has been compiled from sources deemed reliable, and it is accurate to the best of the Author's knowledge; however, the Author cannot guarantee its accuracy and validity and cannot be held liable for any errors or omissions. Changes are periodically made to this book. You must consult your doctor or get professional medical advice before using any of the suggested remedies, techniques, or information in this book.

Upon using the information contained in this book, you agree to hold harmless the Author from and against any damages, costs, and expenses, including any legal fees potentially resulting from the application of any of the information provided by this guide. This disclaimer applies to any damages or injury caused by the use and application, whether directly or indirectly, of any advice or information presented, whether for breach of contract, tort, negligence, personal injury, criminal intent, or under any other cause of action.

You agree to accept all risks of using the information presented inside this book. You need to consult a professional medical practitioner in order to ensure you are both able and healthy enough to participate in this program.

Table of contents

Introduction 1

Chapter 1: For France To Be Restored To Its Glory 8

Chapter 2: Joan Of Ar The French Victory 1429-1453... 26

Chapter 3: Jan Of Ar The Battles Of The Loire Valley 40

Chapter 4: The Coronation Of Charles And Its Aftermath.. 56

Chapter 5: The Brutal Trial 68

Chapter 6: The Inquisition...................... 70

Chapter 7: The Exoneration Of John Of Arc 83

Chapter 8: The Maid 94

Chapter 9: War Hero 105

Chapter 10: The Heretic 144

Chapter 11: Childhood 162

Conclusion 183

Introduction

France was at a crossroads of crisis. In some ways, it was nearing the brink of collapse and barely able to stand in the face of the attacks from a foreign power in the course of a long conflict that even changed Frenchman into Frenchman. The territories of the country were split across various factions. The French who was the heir to the crown of an old-mad dead king was removed from the throne and moved towards the south, whereas the king of England's infancy and his guardians held an enclave in northern territories and beginning an even stronger move southward.

In 1429 and, for the first time in the Hundred-Year War. The English held the upper hand. They had won numerous important victories, often in the face of unimaginable odds, and they had land to show for it, including Paris. They also formed an alliance with a formidable group of Frenchmen, known as the Burgundians and had signed an advantageous agreement that was meant to ensure their claim to the French monarchy for England. The heir to Charles VI of France, the Dauphin Charles of Valois Charles VI of France and the Dauphin Charles of Valois was adamant that the throne was his rightfully however, in reality it was no different from "The King of Bourges," as he was often referred to as in mockery after the court he ruled within the capital city. He was not even crowning according to centuries of French customs that required him to be presented with holy oil at Reims' Cathedral of Reims in territories that were not under his control.

The Dauphin was, as it was stated, was exhausted from fighting. He had difficulty bringing his troops together. The army was down and out of sorts after suffering numerous losses. The city of Orleans was in a state of siege for many months. The French garrison within was being depleted by the chain of English fortresses around the city on three sides and the chances of sending reinforcements that would be able to break the siege looked inadequate. The collapse of Orleans and the battle of

Orleans, which appeared to be imminent, would provide the English forces an ideal position from which to attack the French grip on the south.

A fanciful heroine emerged out of the blue to turn the course of events. A teenager - determined, passionate, persistent, and so confident of her divine destiny called on the fortress of his in Chinon. She wanted soldiers. She wished to serve her God with her daphin. In return, she gave her victory. Through her design or her own being, her existence also gave her nationmen strength and hope.

At first, it appeared she could offer nothing beyond her words. However, her words soon were supported by evidence of prophecies being fulfilled and capabilities that wouldn't be accessible to a single "Maid" in Domremy and an unexpectedly powerful speech to defend her bellefs... Then the proof became legend. Legends enthralled her fellow citizens and frightened their adversaries. The re-energized rally ultimately allowed her country to win victory even though she was not alive to witness it.

It was a shame that was over to the "Maid." She only got two years of public life when she was taken prisoner, ransomed to enemies, detained then charged, tried, and executed. Her amazing beauty was cut short by the blazes of the pyre used for execution. It was reported that her body was burnt three times before her ashes were dispersed. She was just 19 years old. aged.

Her climb was as swift and swift as the fall. She was a tenant farmer's daughter who was in the same position as the King whom she helped crown but was eventually thrown to her family members. She was untrained, but stood her own against the learned from two different countries. She was eloquent and confident of her divine purpose. She lived her life and lived in the conviction that she was a divine messenger from God But she was executed for being a heretic. A century later she was declared sainthood. She is still an inspirational lightbulb for her nation, to women and to the millions around the world who are a part of her beliefs.

The story happened to Joan of Arc:

"La Pucelle" is the maid "La Pucelle" was a woman who, inspired by the voice of saints, embarked to fulfill a mandate by God to bring her country back to freedom and crown its dauphin King. However, first she had overcome her own prejudices and convince her people to be willing to risk their lives on an uninformed, perhaps mad and inexperienced peasant girl who came from the fields of Domremy.

It was the War Hero, whose feats in breaking the English assault on the strategic city of Orleans was an extremely crucial moment of the Hundred Years of War. Territories were lost to France and her troops were demoralized after several major losses. The dauphin was removed from her position and was rapidly exhausted from fighting and the English were knocking at the doors of French strongholds and made their way south , only to be rejected with La Pucelle with her armies.

The Heretic who was snubbed by her own people, being sold to the enemies of her and tried in a foreign-controlled country and convicted of being as a fraud, was thrown down from the highs of her extraordinary victories, suffered losses, was unable to sustain her political value and had her faith tested. The execution was eventually completed and burned in agony before the cross and her mouth was ringing out pleas to Jesus until her death. When she was only 19 she was "Maid of Orleans" was a victim of the highest cost for her part of God's angelic messenger in the gruesome medieval games played by kings and princes.

The Icon is eventually recognized as a true prophet, her extraordinary achievement of her work and her influence on the people who believed in her, was declared as a saint for hundreds of years in the aftermath of her atrocious execution. She has since transcended her initial purpose of her life. Beyond France she has become an idol to Catholics as well as women and other segments of society. Her work is discussed and studied. Her legend is discussed, dissected and unraveled. Her story continues to draw people the reader in awe and wonder. Her stunning image is nearly always used for various reasons.

It's almost a feat in and of itself. Her most famous feats took just two years, and yet she has remained relevant to thousands of people, for thousands of years later, after her brief and memorable life.

Chapter 1: For France To Be Restored To Its Glory

"One lifetime is the only one we've got, and we live it because we believe that it is worth living. But to lose the things you value and be apathetic this is a fate more dreadful than death."
JAN OF ARC

In the 8th century AD the saintly monk named the Venerable Bede prophesied:
"...by the border of Lorraine. France could be destroyed by one woman, but restored by the virgin."
The legend says that an identical prophecy was made through the legend of the wizard Merlin and was even more ancient than that, in the 6th century. It's interesting that both were English and the maid they mentioned was, Joan of Arc, an ardent woman, lived in Domremy the village of the Duchy of Lorraine in France.

THE HUNDRED YEARS"WAR

T

These perennial foes were fighting battle on the fertile hills and valleys that surrounded Northern France- France and England. Over a century between 1337 and 1353, they engaged in battle. The roots of the conflict go back to the time that the English King had married a French noblewoman, who had been granted the land, especially within Normandy located in Northern France. This war was strongly motivated by politics.

The Edwardian Phase 1337-1360

The King Edward III, who ruled in 1337, was the heir to Aquitaine, the region of Aquitaine through his wedding to an French Heiress. King Edward was granted Aquitaine as the duchy Aquitaine despite the opposition from the King Philip VI of France. The initial stage of the Hundred Years war, lasted almost thirty years beyond the time of this claim. In 1360, at Easter, Edward III of England was forced to abandon his claim to be the King of France. But the two sides reached a compromise. John II had to sign a treaty to allow England to keep Aquitaine and a portion of Calais which was the Northeastern portion of France located close to that English border. While England was not completely out of France the treaty, known as the Treaty of Bretigny, gave France greater area than it had previously.

Caroline Phase 1368-1389 Caroline Phase 1368-1389

As we've discussed, connected in that Edwardian Phase of the Hundred Years The Hundred Years' War Aquitaine was under the control by the English. Aquitaine was the home of Edward III was referred to as"the "Black Prince" who was in charge of tax collection and the oversight for the French who lived in Aquitaine. The prince was given the title as the "Black Prince" due to two factors that included) his black cape and shield and cape, and secondly) his inhumanity towards French farmers and owners of the land in Aquitaine. The Black Prince decided to impose ridiculous taxes due to situation that England was fighting an unrelated conflict with Spain and required money to carry it out. Due to this inequity and the plight of those who were unable to pay the bill, the French people in the land demanded Charles V, the The King of France, Charles V, for assistance. They needed help urgently.

The English were not interested, so Charles V built up his army and ready for combat. The French employed a completely different military strategy from what they before. The strategy was referred to as"The "Fabian" strategy, after the old Roman general named Fabius who led an extensive campaign by destroying the enemy with smaller battles instead of using massive frontal attacks. Because of the French efforts, vast areas of the territory of Aquitaine were restored. The victory was not just through military effort however there was tensions within England and France regarding the succession of their respective thrones when Edward III of England and Charles V of France died and left the thrones to the younger leaders. The kingdoms were run by regents, which is family members who were more involvement in provincial issues rather than fighting. This period was an important the acquisition of land in France but except for Gascony, the provincial region Gascony along with the capital city Calais. It was the Treaty of Leulinghem closed this section of the Hundred Year of War.

The Lancastrian Phase 1415-1429 of the Lancastrian

Joan of Arc was the most popular heroine in the third stage of the Hundred Year of War. The French were in control of Lorraine within the Northeastern region of France which bordered Germany however, it was under the control by the Burgundians. The Burgundians represent their time in the Valois Dynasty, from the 1328 until 1589. in 1415 the bloody battle of Agincourt was fought that changed the dominance of Lorraine from France to England however it was still controlled through the Burgundians. Even though

Charles d'Albret battled courageously to keep the Lorraine region to France but he was slain by the powerful and greedy Henry V of England. Henry V of England. Charles d'Orleans, the courageous Duke who fought alongside d'Albret, was arrested and spent the rest of his time within the confines of an English prison. The duchy where Joan along with her parents resided was under the authority of English monarchs.

Joan of Arc had just turned two when the misfortune came on the couple. Jacques d'Arc, Joan's father was the owner of a house at the heart of the Duchy. It was a gorgeous piece of arable farmland that not one that an English monarch should ever be able to rule.

In front of their home the rivulet ran through the Meuse river. Meuse. Their estate was twenty acres. In the meadows Jacques and his men of labor cultivated oat and rye. When she was older the young Joan enjoyed helping men out in the field occasionally and was the shepherdess. The wool that came from sheep was used to spin. For days, Joan along with her mom, Isabelle (later called "Isabelle Remee") spun the wool into clothes for their five children with 3 boys, 2 girls. Joan was also known as "Jeanne," as they loved to call her, was the youngest of the five.

The Bad Treaty of Troyes 1420

Sure the proud French could have served their country that was left to them since the days during the reign of Charlemagne without the dreadful black Plague and the scandalous interference of Queen Isabeau and the wife of incompetent Charles VI. Her family was Bavarian however she was always loyal to the king Henry V of England and wrote the Treaty of Troyes to please Henry V to please him. This treaty granted the Northern region in France in the name of Henry V and left out the true heir to monarchy, Charles VII. After rumors surfaced about the "convenient" report in which it was claimed that the heir apparent, or "Dauphin2, "Dauphin2," - was unlegitimate, Henry had a rationale to block Charles from taking over the throne following when his father died. Many French believed that the Treaty of Troyes was a massive infringement on the integrity of France. The Northern region in the Loire in France is, of course was the area where Joan of Arc and her family resided.

The political scene was tense in Joan's region due to two political parties that were the "Armagnac faction" and the "Burgundian faction" were at war over the power of King England to regulate the areas of France. The Burgundian faction was more favorable to the English. Her father and mother , as well as their neighbors had long discussions regarding this unfortunate incident. They , along with their neighbors, firmly were of the opinion that France was only for people of the French citizens, and not for the Burgundians and neither the English who came across the English Channel.

Joan's early Heavenly Visitors 1425

Joan was a lover of wandering around their garden with her family and meditate. She adored the bells that rang at night in the church in the village. She was a religious child who went to Mass every day and would spend long hours in prayer. She was a prayer warrior for her family, her friends as well as for France. At night she was on a garden bench at the dusk. The sun's rays was beginning to fade, yet night was still not fully set. The dusk is a mystical space between when sounds and sounds are eerie and blurred by the trick of light and dark. From a distance Joan noticed a faint glow which grew and grew in the misty night air. She was enthralled and observed as a bright glow grew into a shape and a face was carved from the light. There were whispers in the air. It wasn't scary, it was quite peaceful. It gave her a sense of tranquility she'd never experienced before. She was awestruck and amazed. Every day, the vision came back. One day the vision spoke words as

soft as a breeze, yet as powerful like the wind which signals the arrival of an approaching storm. She was feeling as if ought to be scared but it wasn't. It was a beautiful voice, and yet she wasn't sure how she could have known that. A few nights ago, it said to her:
"You have to go to France. You can't stay in the place you are."

In the year of her birth, the duchy in which she resided was Lorraine However, Lorraine was not considered to be part France in the way it been because it was now run by English supreme rulers. The first night she was able to see the figure and it appeared lovely. Joan of Arc came to realize that the figure could be St. Michael the Archangel. How this could be possible was not clear to her but she was certain that it was the truth.

She then asked to go along with him into the divine location where he resides however he refused.

St. Michael came many times more, and at once he told her that more angels from the heavens would visit and assist her. He then told her that she should quit this peaceful woodland garden by the farm of her dad.

Then, the imposing voice said to her:
"You must put up the siege that was laid on Orleans. Orleans. You must go towards Robert de Baudricourt at the castle of Vaucouleurs The captain of the fortress. The Captain would provide you with the men you need to go with you."

In response to her claim that she was just a weak girl who had no idea about commanding men in war, he promised him that she'd be able to count on other saints of the heavenly realm to guide her along the road.

There were three saintly figures. She pleaded for their names and they replied that they were Saint. Catherine of Alexandria, the holy martyr of the enchanting country from Egypt as well as the saint St. Margaret of Antioch, the martyr of the Byzantine World. They were the greatest Catholic saints from Christendom. While they were there, Joan was inundated with an euphoria and reason. Joan wasn't certain at first what the reason was but the saints appeared so beautiful and yet real that she was never able to doubt the things she witnessed.

Joan was aware that a bloody conflict was raging in the area around her. But, at one point, this terrible war was heard in a scream of terror and the roar of guns and cannons. The ground was shaken by the rumbling of horses' hooves that were a few miles away. A great ache struck her in the once tranquil community of Domremy. Her parents raced into their tiny home, take her and her children in tears, claiming that their modest homes in the town's centre were in flames. In the midst of the chaos, a gang of enraged soldiers fields. In a state of chaos her parents, her and siblings packed up whatever clothing as well as food items they were able to carry, and fled to the city of Chateauneuf.

The Dauphin

Charles VII of France had recently claimed the throne he deserved in 1422. But Henry VI, the Henry VI, the King of England, Henry VI, claimed the Duchy of York for himself. To protect Charles VII's safety, advisers advised him to remain in Chinon. Chinon located just south of Orleans. France was so damaged by the Hundred Year's War as well as the threat of encroaching by the Black Plague which had entered France and spread throughout France, that Chinon was regarded as the most secure place to stay.

To stop in order to prevent the English in their move further South To stop the English from moving further South, Garrison commander Robert de Baudricourt had his troops in the defensive zone to defend the new King. The situation was becoming more dire and Joan was informed by the saints who had appeared in her dreams that she actually was the bride of the legend that was to save France. Joan became so determined and determined to follow their orders that she even told her father that she was planning be a soldier. He was shocked. Her mother and he demanded that she get married just like the rest of French girls of her age.

The year 1427 was the time that Joan fled and was able to find refuge at a relative's house in the city of Vaucouleurs. Being impressed by the genuineness of the child her mother, Durand Laxart, agreed to transport her to the Commander Robert de Baudricourt at the King's residence. In Vaulcouleurs the first time, she was received by Jean de Metz, a servant of Robert de Baudricourt, the garrison commander. De Metz was surprised when she requested to meet with the King and recommended him to de Baudricourt. Jean de Metz and his companion squire, Bertrand Poulengy, continued to talk to her. But her manner of conduct impressed them and they concluded that she was serious enough to warrant an audience. They also took her to their commanding officer.

As she was heard by de Baudricourt appeared humble. She was just a an innocent girl dressed with the serge red dress typical of the peasant. In a resolute manner, she informed her that she was going to bring the King victory over English. He was frenziedly asking her who's command she was heading on this mission of great importance.
"He is King in Heaven,"
she said. He laughed and ordered her removed.

Joan propagated the news regarding her cause to people living in the area, and gained a lot of attention. As time passed, they were convinced that she could indeed deliver a message from God. After being back to her home for a few days and begging her parents to forgive her and then shared her thoughts with them. They were frightened for her, yet they understood the strength Joan was determined. The English tried to then put their city Orleans under the threat of siege. It was 1429 when Joan returned to de Baudricourt but he refused to meet her. After her third attempt, she was able to meet de Baudricourt regarding an audience with the King, France was then undergoing the ravages of a siege at Orleans which was one of the major cities within the Northeastern region. De Baudricourt was in a mental state that was different at the time , and was listening to her attentively. While they talked, Joan predicted that the French were likely to lose control over Orleans without her permission to intervene. She asked again to meet the King. When she spoke to de Baudricourt, she said:

"I alone, and only one other person, whether it is King, Duke or the daughter of King of Scots will be able to restore the Kingdom of France. I'm not obligated to be soldiers, however, I am required to follow my purpose as my Lord has ordained me to carry out this task."

Robert de Baudricourt then left the room and returned with a priest in order to determine whether she was being influenced to evil spirits, or good spirits. After examining her, returned and stated she was sincere and trustworthy.

After being quizzed by a few more ecclesiastical officials, Joan was finally given permission to visit the King. After which - finally she was led to the room in which she was to meet with King Charles, Charles had disguised himself as courtiers. Despite this, Joan recognized him immediately and knelt down to his feet.
"God provide you with a blissful life, my sweet King."
She told him. Charles was shocked, but amused and curious. He secretly thought that she might be delusional but. While they talked but she also told him a secret only known to herself. After hearing that the secret, his face changed. The King felt

the young lady had been chosen through God for the purpose of saving France.

In the end, Jean de Metz and Bertrand de Poulengy presented her with the modified uniform of a soldier with a banner embroidering the figure of Christ who held the entire world in his arms. Two angels were on each side of the figure of Christ.

Robert de Baudricourt also gave her the sword. The group was led by team of soldiers, led by Jean de Metz and Bertrand de Poulengy.

1 Charles VI experienced periodic episodes of madness and was occasionally in a state of confusion.
2. The name "Dauphin" is conferred to the son of the king. of the king. they consider him to be as the heir apparent.

Chapter 2: Joan Of Ar The French Victory 1429-1453

"I do not fear... I was made to be a professional."
JAN OF ARC

It was the final phase of the Hundred Year's War which was the most infamous war of all time. Joan of Arc was the most famous military commander France has ever had. A lot of injustices had been imposed on France in the years since 1337. Its inhabitants were oppressed, beaten and starved until they were forced to fight to ensure their survival in order to rid their beautiful nation of the ruthless overlords, the English. They fought for many years, fought by the Black Plaque in the 1300's and re-established their farms and rebuilt their towns repeatedly. They required a savior. However, who would have thought their savior would come in the shape of a 19-year-old girl. But, she was able to harness all the power of heaven, and the force of her spirit.

Her troops accompany her as she traveled through the treacherous area that was Northern France, now occupied by a rogue army of English soldiers. The destination they chose was Orleans where 30,000 inhabitants hid within the city's walls, afraid of the being encircled English army. The people were furious that the Dauphin abandoned them, and it was apparent. They were running exhausted of food and supplies. They even tried to come to a peace agreement with the English however, the offer was not accepted.

When Joan was at the French camp in the city of Blois just 35 miles from Orleans she was surprised to find there were French soldiers were playing with prostitutes. Joan stood up and ordered the prostitutes to leave. When she saw the banner and the French troops that were along with Joan her, the soldiers followed her orders and were brought back to their proper place. Then she was joined by her commanders, Jean de Dunois and Etienne de Vignolles. They were and was also referred to as "La Hiring."

Joan of Arc planned on returning to French control over Northern France starting with the city of Orleans and then planned to move Northward towards Rheims. It was in Rheims she wished to be the Dauphin to honor his coronation which was a prophesy she later shared with him personally.

The ORLEANS CAMPAIGN
From March to Orleans

F
during her travels, Joan and her soldiers were carrying provisions, small boats as well as food to the beleaguered inhabitants of Orleans as well as their

military gear. They walked across the fields in Touraine and set up their tents for the night. The journey was long trek. Despite the fact that it was an occupied territory the group was not met with opposition. The next early morning Joan stated that she would like to go into Orleans by way of towards the North However, she was prevented by her her leaders. When they first visited the city, Joan observed that a rising Loire River lay between her forces and the bastilles of Orleans. The river was very high and it was able to flood the plains that surrounded it. Joan decided to make it through, whether it was flood or not flood , so they turned to southwards to the South under her guidance and took in a circular route to reach the crossing. A contingent of French warriors needed to split off and engage in small fights with the English fortress in the city to get into. As night fell and they were able to enter with the darkness obscuring their eyes the boats were sailed and sct sail

towards Orleans. Although the wind seemed to be against their sails, the river were calm when Joan of Arc approached.
Entry into Orleans

Joan as well as de Dunois contacted the English commanding officer at Orleans and requested to allow humanitarian assistance to be delivered in the city. The English occasionally allow it in times of war. He was in agreement. Then, de Dunois and her knights went into the city. The word spread quickly. Many people came to her, and soldiers distributed food and other items. She then assured the crowd with the words,
"My Lord has sent me to assist this wonderful community of Orleans. Have faith in God And if you are able to do so that - you'll be delivered from the wrath of your foes."
Although the English let the humanitarian help to go out, they used the chance to yell jeers at Joan and label her a witch, a wicked witch and

"cowgirl." Joan distributed the food and provisions , afterwards, she spent a few days at the residence of Jacques Boucher, the Treasurer of the City.

Following her brief stay, the English let her and her soldiers to leave without injury. They were scared of her powers. Joan was then exiled from Orleans but it was only a temporary. In the evening, she to circle around Orleans and checked out the fortresses that were near the city's walls as well as the gates that protected the English. There were anywhere from five and six fortresses. Some fortresses were taken down since the materials of one fortification was required to protect other important locations in the vicinity of Orleans.

Assault on St. Loup

The city's first fortress was situated at the Eastern Gate into the city in the vicinity that is St. Loup. Joan was sleeping near the fortress in the evening, only to be awakened by the sound of her angelic voice. When she awoke, she found that her soldiers had already fought with the English who were in the countryside , but they hadn't told her. She was furious and even criticized the soldiers for shielding her from fighting.

"Will you not let me know that your blood from France is being spilled? Get me my horse!"

When she met her soldiers when she rode into the midst of her white horse and saw how the French were weakened. A church within the city wall was partially destroyed. When her French soldiers were able to see her, a huge celebration erupted and brought them renewed energy. Arrows flew off from the English archers but without success. Further French attacks were launched and by now, they French were outnumbered by the English waiting for reinforcements. The English began to retreat and the French pushed ahead, while Joan and her troops moved forward with their swords, swinging them and launching them into the enemies. They French were under Joan of Arc had won control of the St. Loup gate.

Then, suddenly, Lord John Talbot arrived with English reinforcements. As the battle was at its peak and he sped towards the North and rode up to the fort, and tried to protect his troops. However, upon looking out at the battlefield and seeing many of his troops injured in the wreckage of the church that had been badly damaged and the Church was completely destroyed, he and his troops went to hide out. Joan barred her soldiers from be allowed into the church, in keeping with the sacred principle.

When she left as she was leaving, she sent a message for the Lord Talbot as well as his fellow soldiers:
"You are, O English who have no claim to the kingdom of France The King of

Heaven is directing you, through me Joan the maid. get out of your fortresses, and return to your homeland, and If you don't comply, I'll cause a ruckus that will be remembered forever."

Lord Talbot was defeated by the troops of a woman. He was angry and humiliated.

Assault on Augustins

The English had Fortifications in a variety of locations. After witnessing the bravery of the young woman in St. Loup, many of the French residents of the city that was under siege Orleans formed militias of their own, built the river using improvised pontoon bridges, and joined her. However they were unable to defend themselves, it was the English took down the bridge.

One of the many fortifications in the South of Orleans lay in the Tourelles-Boulevart-Augustins area. Joan took her army towards to the Augustins bastion.

They met with a ferocious opposition on their flanks by the English. Then , a roar was heard from the bastille in Augustins and Joan directed her troops there. In the belief that it was an indication of a French retreat and retreat, and the English garrison commander William Glasdale and his men were chased by the garrison commander William Glasdale. Joan then shrewdly turned and confronted him head-on. She began to raise her banner, she shouted
"In God's name" God,"
They became terrified at the ferocity of Joan. Since Joan and her army attacked them in this manner that they turned and rode along on their horses to the fortress of Boulevart. She was tempted to pursue but her knight Baron Gilles de Rais turned her back towards the Augustins. The fight continued throughout the day. Near the conclusion of the day Joan was injured on her foot. Despite her discomfort, she carried on as she was not injured enough to be

dismounted. In the evening the bastille had fallen into the hands of French.

She was removed from the battlefield to recuperate, and her other commanders encouraged her to stay in recovery during the battle to come further South in the next day. She refused to do so, and the next morning, she got her horse saddled and rode it down to the fortifications in Tourelles. When the French people saw her doing that, they clapped.

Assault on The Tourelles and Boulevart

During these combats in the course of the battles, they saw the English leader, William Glasdale, moved his troops away from Boulevart redoubt, to redoubt located at Tourelles. He was waiting for Joan as well as her troops. They were waiting. French military from Orleans who were assisting the French army in repairing their pontoon bridge, and had were planning to aid Joan by launching an artillery assault from a small island on the Loire River.

The fort's foundations in the Tourelles were very strong as was de Dunois and the French soldiers fought for a full day trying to destroy the foundations. Joan was able to meditate and was able to receive an uncanny voice telling her that the next day blood would flow from her body over her breasts.

After she had returned, Joan noted that Glasdale and his men were in the Tourelles and had left protecting the redoubt at Boulevart. In a bid to take advantage of this, Joan and her regiment returned to the fortress of Boulevart that they had left earlier. She gathered several ladders, and set them against the huge wall. She herself set up an incline and began climbing up. When she reached the top the ladder, an arrow struck her right over her left shoulder and she was lowered and slowly transported into a litter to recuperate.

As they realized the fact that Joan was injured, French morale sank and the English started to feel more confident. But, Joan had her wound temporary covered and was able to her troops. It worked. All her soldiers were able to climb the ladders and ran over the wall, and took the fortress in Boulevart.

In the following days, Joan along with the French forces moved towards the Tourelles in preparation for the final attack. The moment Glasdale as well as the English emerged from the fortress to confront the French the drawbridge gave the way. The English soldiers fell into the deep moat including Glasdale who drowned.

The French army quickly restored the drawbridge and crossed it and sacked the fortress. The following night, Tourelles had been taken by French. The English lost more than 1,000 men. 600 were taken in prison.

Orleans was free!

Chapter 3: Jan Of Ar The Battles Of The Loire Valley

"I prefer to die than commit a crime that I recognize as unrighteous, or go against God's plan."
Joan of Arc

The city of Orleans was surrounded by numerous areas. of Orleans along the Loire River now were under French dominance. The main city that served as the main entrance point to Southern France is Orleans and Joan of Arc had helped in French army retake of English control. Orleans was located just east of Chinon, the castle. Chinon in the area where Charles VII, the Dauphin was residing. Joan of Arc had promised Charles VII that he would be crowning King in Rheims however the French were required to manage all of the Loire areas first. Rheims is situated in Northern France which the English had ruled from when they signed the Treaty of Troyes.

THE SOUTHERN LIRE CAMPAIGN

T
Three towns of a small size were situated in strategically placed areas south from the Loire River - Jargeau, Beaugency and Patay.

Battle of Jargeau

Duke John II Alencon, Commander de Dunois and their soldiers were accompanied by Joan towards Jargeau. Jargeau at the end of summer in 1429. They carried with them a captured cannon from Orleans and 600 soldiers equipped with bowmen, lances and artillery, as well as a force of 2800 additional troops. The troops were joined by additional French soldiers, including some under the command of Captain La hire, when they fought Jargeau. Prior to the fight they sent a few soldiers to protect the suburbs.

The English were under the direction by the Duke of Suffolk, William de la Pole. De la Pole had been promised some reinforcements.

In that town's wall French troops dragged out the cannon and instantly destroyed one tower. Joan of Arc realized that the French far outnumbered the English which is why she offered Suffolk the chance to surrender and avoid bloodshed. As if he believed that the reinforcements he promised would arrive on time and he would not accept.

"Advance, gentle Duke,"
He called out Joan to Alencon and he hadn't been fighting alongside Joan from Arc and wasn't sure what to think of her.
"To the attack!"
He was still hesitant - possibly because she was a woman and she pleaded with him:

"Doubt not! It is the time to be sure that God Wills! God assists those who assist themselves. Dear Duke, do you feel afraid!"

In the wake of her determination voice, he started the attack. Joan and the French soldiers Joan as well as soldiers of the French soldiers then sat on their ladders on the walls, and then climbed up the wall. As the French gained entry to the city the Joan's helmet was struck by a stone thrown at her by an English soldier. The impact caused her to tumble to the floor. She immediately stood up and yelled to them.
"On friends, on! in less than an hour we'll have these!"

The French victory was a simple one The French won easily, and Joan was right when she predicted the outcome. Furthermore Duke of Suffolk was also taken prisoner. Duke of Suffolk was imprisoned.

From that moment to the present from that point, Duke John II Alencon discovered that she was a courageous and strong woman, who was worthy of his unwavering commitment. He was never hesitant again.

Battle of Meung-sur-Loire

Meung-sur-Loire was a tiny town located on the Loire River. It was surrounded by large walls around, and there were fortifications constructed by the English close to the walls to deter the return of the French army. The bridge was over the river as well as an castle. Although the town was tiny however, it played a significant role in the war since it gave the English the ability to access Central as well as Southern France.

The forces of Joan of Arc and her commanders, La Hire and a new commander named the young Jean Ponton, staged a combative front over

the fortifications. They quickly destroyed them by climbing their ladders, then took on the castle. It took them less than an hour to take over the castle and expel the English from the castle. However Lord John Talbot, the powerful English commander there fled.
Battle of Montepilloy

It was a minor incident however the castle was the home of the notorious Duke of Bedford. When the French arrived at the castle the Duke was already gone and was on his journey to the adjoining regions. He was Duke of Bedford was an active participant in the Hundred Years War and was in a state of anger when the girl was trying to retake lands were conquered by him earlier. Bedford seemed more interested in the political system of England.

The fighting lasted two days, however - because of the stubbornness by the French army, they English was forced to leave. Today, only a tiny portion of the castle walls remains.

Battle of Beaugency

Prior to the time that the French attacked the suburbs of Meung-sur-Loire the French seized the bridge that crossed the Loire River. Meung was a town. Meung was not subjected to an French attack, however its castle was later surrendered.

Lord John Talbot, who had been in the Church's area of St. Loup had left there and had now joined his troops at Beaugency. Joan Duchess John II Alencon as well as the French army marched towards that town. In the beginning they took control of the town. Then, the French assumed control of the bridge crossing the river, and then moved into the citadel, not being in the city itself. The castle could be the place where they would locate Talbot. The French were right in their analysis and Talbot and his army were found in the castle. The French attacked the castle with a series of volleys of wrathful artillery fire.

When he heard from his scouts English reinforcements were set come in Paris, Alencon sent the English to surrender, promising safety in the event of Beaugency. They were unharmed when they left.
Battle of Patay

Patay was situated on a plain that was wide. In Patay there was a place where the English kept a garrison, and were there for a while. In reality, the bread they ate there consume was damp. The English who had been promised reinforcements under the command of Commander Fastolf were also present.

Captain La Hire was in Joan in leading the French army towards Patay. La Hire heard a shout from the English who had been in the area for so long, they knew

they would be wary the long wait. La Hire looked at Joan and said:
"Shall we take on them?"
"Have you nice spurs Prince?" Joan asked.
"Why?" he asked, "Will they make us leave?"
"These English are ours - they're lost. They'll fly. If they do, they'll need strong spurs. Forward!"
Joan called out.

Joan later instructed her new commander Jean Ponton, to hold back. Initially, this frightened him however, he complied.

The vanguard troops, under La Hire who was in charge, whipped their horses with such force that the English believed that they thought the French were speeding away in a frenzied rush. Fastolf, the commander of in the English advance guard, panicked and fled. Joan's tactics was successful! Talbot who was following from a distance, was in a state of anger however, the English soldiers were effectively divided, and Talbot did not have enough soldiers left to put up a decent defense.

Joan was then able to get over her second force of attack, and exclaimed,
"Follow me!"
Jean Ponton and his men were advancing towards Talbot's troops, attacking and slashing the English adversaries as they defeated them.

Joan ran forward and she raised her sword high, and turned her back to her men, and she said:
"The thanks go to God. He has struck with a heavy blow today. In a thousand years , 1,000 years - English power won't be able to recover from this defeat (defeat)!"

Talbot was stunned and puzzled. What was the way this young woman get through that? He then stated:
"My thoughts spin like a wheel of a potter. I'm not sure where I amor what I am doing A witch, driven in fear, not through force, as Hannibal and Hannibal, represses our soldiers and conquers."

When the English left, Joan looked upon the field of Patay that was now stained by blood. After spotting the dying English soldier on the battlefield, she kneeled close to him and held his head while whispering words of sympathy and sorrow and tears streaming through her eyes. That's what happens when nations turn to violence rather than treaties to settle their disputes.

The history of the area has documented that around 2500 English died in that meadow. Just 100 Frenchmen were killed.

MARTCH to RHEIMS

T
Dauphin was awed and thrilled by the successes at Orleans and in the Loire Valley. Dauphin then planned to hold his coronation in Orleans. Joan however, was aware that the coronation would be held in Rheims to show the French citizens that in fact the French have now got their country of love back from the English. Charles VII was already on his journey to Rheims when Joan of Arc contacted him and made arrangements to meet him on the Benedictine Abbey in the Loire Valley. Joan visited and talked to the Dauphin to convince him God had told her that Charles VII would be crowned at Rheims. He finally was willing to accept.

Joan was now forced to move Northward. The area was filled by English fortresses, however Joan was not worried. She along wIth the Dauphin along with his army moved through the region without firing shot. Joan rode alongside the Dauphin along with de Dunois, La Hire, Jean Ponton, and other people. The Dauphin had his own army comprising 12,000 soldiers.

In the time, increasing French troops and soldiers flocked to join Joan as well as the Dauphin. There were around 70,000 people at the time. This was in an area called"The "Glen." There were two battles occurred in the area One was in Bonny-sur-Loire and the other at Sant-Fargeau. The two were easily taken down.

In the town of Auxerre The French were met with resistance when Anglo-affiliated Burgundian forces were unable to open their gates. Since they were not English in their own right and were Burgundians their mayor requested to remain neutral , and they was granted this request. Then, the Dauphin and the

other French forces were encamped overnight.
Siege of Troyes

On the 9th of July, in the city of Troyes where the crucial treaty was signed in 1420 There was a garrison of English regiments. Joan sent in a messenger demanding surrender. The English commander refused to accept the request. The numerous English forces took over the city and placed the city under siege during five consecutive days. The fifth day was the day they gave up. It was the smartest option they could have made since the French significantly outnumbered them. There was also a deal on the French prisoners that they held. These prisoners were released, and incorporated with the French march towards Rheims.
From there, it's onwards to Rheims

Paris lies to the Southwest however, it was under the control of the Burgundian faction that was under the direction under the leadership of "Philip the Good," who wasn't well-named. Realizing that the French were making advancements, he stopped fighting the Burgundian claim that was nothing more than an unpopular rebel group. Duke Philip was then exiled and began a march Southwest towards Paris prior to his arrival by the Dauphin.

The fortress of Chalons-en-Champagne then made their doors open to French and a truce flag was displayed! Joan was able to blow her bugles and then they marched through the town, to cheers of celebration towards the town. Charles the Dauphin was also in the march along with Sir John II Alencon and Commander de Dunois. The people and the clergy paid an obeisance towards the Dauphin and urged them to stay the night. There were still a few English from the Burgundian group and they stood at a distance while the royals arrived and stayed until the early morning of the 16th of the 16th of July 1429.

The next date, Joan sent a treaty proposal to Philip who was the Duke of Burgundy who acted in behalf of the English King. The sister of Joan was his father, the Duke of Bedford who commanded the English army in France. While he was French but he was also allied with the English in this time of the Hundred Year's War. Two weeks later The Duke of Bedford himself refused to accept the offer to a truce, and he responded and not Joan of Arc instead to Dauphin. In mockery, he stated:
"You are able to seduce and manipulate the insane and depend on the help from the superstitious, unreliable or even a notorious and deranged woman who dresses wearing a suit and unruly."

Chapter 4: The Coronation Of Charles And Its Aftermath

"Children believe that people are sometimes hung because they speak the truth."

JAN OF ARC

The entry of the royal family into Rheims 1429.

Charles VII and his entourage were joined by Joan of Arc and Duke John II Alencon and thousands of French troops. Joan's father was present at the ceremony too. He was so happy for his daughter. The spires of the grand cathedral of Rheims stood in front of them. The soldiers of the previous Burgundian group gathered to welcome the king, as did the people. A huge cheer was heard from the crowd.

Charles was at the altar and then seated himself on the throne they had made for Charles. Then Regnault Archbishop of Chartres put the crown on his head. In

triumph, the trumpets rang out. Everyone shouted "
"Long Live Charles!" Charles!"

While most coronations are marked by a lot of celebration and ceremony however, those which took place at the period were more quiet than the majority. The English were still holding the territories of Paris, Calais, and Gascony. There was a Duke from Bedford was in the area and so was Philip from Burgundy.

BATTLES TO WIN the entirety of France
Battle of Lagnyan. Battle of Lagny

The town of Lagny was situated near Paris and was in which the English were inseparable. A few of those who supported the Burgundian faction in France remain in occupied areas of France such as the village of Lagny. They had to be evicted to make way for Paris to an army of the French Army. The majority of French troops at Rheims had dispersedand Joan needed more troops to continue the battle. Charles provided only a tiny group however Joan determined to prevail in spite of odds. It was the English Burgundian, Franquet d'Arras was a person with a reputation that was not so great among his fellow English and Joan was able to capture him. After that, the English forces encamped in Lagny surrendered. The Dauphin was declared King and the English were demotivated by that and therefore didn't put in their all efforts to keep hold of to the Lagny regardless of the fact English forces were outnumbered by the French.

Battle of Paris Battle of Paris

In the month of September 1429 in 1429, in 1429, Duke Philip of Burgundy had fled from Rheims in the event that the Dauphin was preparing to visit the city for the coronation. The plan was to boost Paris by deploying more English troops.

Joan of Arc and the other troops needed to get rid of France of foreigners before Charles could take complete control of his country. Joan of Arc, Charles VII, Duke John II of Alencon, Jean de Brosse, La Hire as well as other excellent French commanders marched towards Paris. The units of the military split in order to control the area around Paris as well. Charles VII gave Joan the instruction to lead the assault on Paris within the city itself. the Duke Philip of Burgundy and his army awaited her arrival.

The city itself was surrounded by massive stone walls that were manned by English soldiers who were who were stationed on the walls' parapets. There was a large moat that was surrounded by a drawbridge prior to that gate. Joan and her men swarmed across the bridge that ran through the moat. They were hit with volley after volley bows fired by the well-trained English crossbowmen. Many were wounded and sank into the water.

Then Joan was badly injured in her thigh with an arrow shot from an archery crossbow. In a resolute manner, her soldiers carried her across the bridge to attend to her.

The King Charles VII only had about 10,000 Frenchmen to conquer the city, while the English Duke was equipped with thirty-three thousand. Due to these massive forces and the overwhelming force of they were defeated by the French were defeated and the King Charles found himself forced to declare the retreat.

Victory came, but it was much later however it happened after Joan of Arc's demise.
Charles: The King Charles"Lost Faith"

After the defeat to Paris, Charles effectively gave all hope of conquering the entirety of France. Charles was often unsure at times , and was less than competent. Additionally, historians believed there was jealousy towards Joan of Arc, who appeared to be more well-known than he was. At the time, the kings and queens were always remain vigilant to prevent others from trying to take their thrones. Even although Joan was female, Charles became unsettled about her. While he wasn't in frequent contact with Joan but he did reply to her messages for support.

The Siege of Saint-Pierre-le-Moutier

In England there were two conflicting families that were internecine - The Yorks along with the Lancastrians. While they engaged in battle in England, some of the Lancastrian-affiliated troops had regained control of some of the French towns in Northern France including Saint-Pierre-le-Moutier. In November of 1429, Joan, having recovered from her leg wound, again marched on Saint-Pierre-le-Moutier near the Loire River. She had her bodyguard Jean d'Aulon wIth her and she fought alongside him along with the other men. The town was fortified heavily and was surrounded by a deep moat. Her first attack was defeated by Lancastrian forces, however Joan had no choice but to fight. Following the initial assault and the commander Jean d'Aulon was slightly wounded but was able to take part in an attack counter-insurgency. After a second attack, Joan of Arc and her formidable French warriors prevailed.

Following her win, the queen was elevated to the throne by King Charles and gladly accepted the award. Following that, Joan told those closest to her that she was ennobled.
"Before two years have passed, I'll die a brutal death."
The Siege of La Charite

La Charite had a large fortification that was constructed during the time of the English who conquered its territory in the year 1423. It was the Dauphin, Charles VII, was keen to return it to French dominance, therefore the Dauphin was sent Joan of Arc and her troops to the area to take the fortification. Joan's troops were exhausted by this time and were was stricken by frigid temperatures at the time of this, in 1429, the year of winter. She wrote to the Dauphin seeking additional provisions and reinforcements. As she waited for the arrival of the Dauphin the troops, she and her soldiers employed their artillery to fight those English in the fort. The inhabitants of the nearby villages provided supplies and artillery to assist her while she waited for her arrival.

After about a month, Joan of Arc and her men realized that the battle would be a waste of time and were forced to leave the battle.

Siege of Compiegne

The year was 1430. In Chapter 1 of this book, There were 2 French factions that dominated Northeastern France The Armagnac faction, which backed France in the region, and the Burgundian faction, which backed England. It was Compiegne that had been as well as Northern France, had been allies together with Burgundians. But after Charles VII was crowned, they changed their allegiance and paid the king a rousing tribute. However the Philip of Burgundy, Duke Philip of Burgundy brought them back and they restored their loyalties to England.

It was in the lead-up to this fight that Joan was given a second premonition by her by her voice. When she was praying they informed her that she'd be taken prisoner in the next few hours. She didn't discuss it with her fellow commanders.

Joan along with the commander Guillaume de Flavy, d'Aulon as well as

Jean Ponton attempted to storm into the town. The French were initially repelled but Joan prepared for a counter-attack and occupied a spot on the French rear guard of the army.

The counter-attack of her was successful, and the battle for Compiegne culminated in an French victory. A few English who were present at Compiegne retreated and left while others remained within the town. Joan of Arc pursued those who were retreating, whereas de Flavy remained at Compiegne to act as the town's Governor. There are some differences among Middle Age historians, but some believed the fact that de Flavy betrayed France. The reason was that a lot of French citizens were trying to get out of Compiegne. Joan and her army were rushing towards Compiegne to defend it in the fight within. Then, the Burgundians closed off the entrance to the town, by lifting the drawbridge. An uncontrollable skirmish ensued that was triggered by the English soldiers hidden in the fields just outside of the town. Due to the drawbridge being closed, Joan couldn't enter the town. In the meantime, she was slowly prevented from entering by hostile Burgundian soldiers who stood behind her. Then she turned around to face them.

The Capture from Joan of Arc

According to an 15th Century eyewitness account of Perceval de Cagny who rode under Duke d'Aulon. She was able to resist with force. In the midst of her distress Joan's troops rushed to help. After that, de Cagny stated that about six of the enemy Burgundians came up to her horse and forced her off of its back. A English archer took her cape, put her down onto the hard ground. He then picked her up , and placed her over his horse. D'Aulon was also taken prisoner.

The English transported Joan up to Beaurevoir Castle along with d'Aulon.

There are reports in Medieval writings that Joan ran off from the top in the castle but not as a suicide attempt but rather in an attempt to escape. The source of these stories are not clear about the way that she did not suffer any injuries but she was captured and taken to the castle in Rouen. The beautiful woman was transported to a cell chained on her legs and arms, and put in a cage made of iron. Rouen was under the control of the ecclesiastical authorities and therefore, they were able to be relied upon.

It was a custom at the time to offer ransom for the most notable prisoners of war. But, due to reasons for which the stories are not clear the Charles, the King Charles offered no ransom.

Chapter 5: The Brutal Trial

"You claim to be my judge. I'm not sure whether you are, but be careful not to make me feel guilty, as you'd put yourself in danger."

JEAN OF ARC

Joan of Arc, despite her achievements in promoting the common cause of the nation of France she was not without her critics. Of course there were those who believed that the English were seeking revenge for humiliating victories won by women However, English (and French) civil law did not support trial for war prisoners. Joan had been legally recognized as a war prisoner since she was captured in Compiegne during the battle. But, the rules regarding war had the potential to be thrown out when she was tried by the Church authorities. In 1431, the English changed the rules to ensure to get rid of the unfortunate maiden. This was mainly due to the brutal efforts of John Duke of Bedford.

He was a conqueror of many French towns to protect the English and was astonished by the accomplishment of a young lady. The Duke informed officials that the motives for being tried in The Catholic Church might be a form of heresy. A lot of Catholics and clerical officials believed that she wasn't just an heretic but a witch.

Chapter 6: The Inquisition

To test a person's character to determine if a person is a saint, the Church established an organ called the Inquisition to test a person in early in the Middle Ages. These ecclesiastical courts were where subjects were questioned to judge their adherence to Church doctrine as well as their faith. Philip Duke of Burgundy made arrangements to have her heard in one of the courts. He was able engage the help from Peter Cauchon, the Bishop of Beauvais. Cauchon was a controversial figure due to his brutality and vengeance. He even been barred from Paris due to it. He was resident in England. Because of being influenced by Philip, Duke of Philip, Cauchon was permitted to return to Paris and was appointed to the University of Paris to monitor the interrogation process of Joan of Arc. He was Dr. Jean Beaupere was the prosecutor during the trial. Beaupere was also a victim of his own orthodoxy tested by the Catholic

Church during the time. He was a close friend of Peter Cauchon and - as Cauchon was also famous for his rigor. Additionally, Beaupere had strong connections to the political system of Henry VI of England. She would be in their presence alongside 30 Doctors from Theology.

On the 21st day of February 1431 she was brought to the courtroom. After the preliminary proceedings were completed by Dr. Beaupere, Dr. Beaupere questioned her regarding the "voices" she'd said she had heard. A shortened version of the questioning:

Beaupere "From where did those voices originate?"

Joan: "I heard the (first) voice coming from my right toward to the church."

Beaupere "Was your voice supported by the bright lighting?"

Joan: "Seldom did I hear the voice without seeing a brilliant light. The light was from the same direction like the voice and it was generally bright."

The Beaupere singer: "What did you think this voice that spoke to you was like?"

Joan: "It seemed to me to be a beautiful voice. I believe it was sent for me to hear by God. When I heard it for the third time I realized it was being the angel's voice."

In the same session, Beaupere asked for additional details:

Joan: "The voice told me to start a siege in Orleans."

Beaupere "Was this all?"

Joan: "The same voice directed me that it was time to travel to Vaulcouleurs in order for Robert de Baudricourt, captain of the area and that he would provide soldiers to accompany me during my travels."

The questions appeared to be biased in the questions were carefully designed in order to frighten her up or uncover irregularities. Certain questions were changed and then asked again to meet the same objective. There weren't any inconsistent statements in her testimony.

During the interrogation during the questioning, her confession about disclosing secrets that were private for the King to reveal things which were secret to him only - was brought up. In the course of 5 days they tried to convince Joan to divulge those personal information. As a sign of respect of the King's privacy, she did not divulge the information, and instead stated that they must inquire from the King himself.

They inquired about her wearing a male outfit to which she responded that it was still not the right enough time to transition to female clothes. While it was not considered to be an offense however, the clerics appeared annoyed that she was wearing male attire. It is believed to be an old rule in the Church. However, the main reason why she remained in the same clothes was due to the fact that her jailers were not believed, and she was certain that they'd attempt to sexually assault her if removed the chain mail and armour.

Odd Questions

From 1378 until 1417 There was a schism within the Catholic Church. Between 1307 and 1376, Pope Clement was at Avignon. The papacy was relegated to Rome however, the event led to the creation of a line of popes who were not legitimate in Avignon. When she was asked which pope she believed was the legitimate pope she was asked

"Which is the Pope that you consider to be the real one, he at Avignon or one in Rome?"

When she was first asked that inquiry, Joan responded,
"Are There two?"
Another day and when asked the same question she responded with the same answer as in Rome. It is possible that she knew the political context of the moment, she would have been aware of that split that took place years earlier.

The identical day Joan was asked whether the angels wearing earrings! Then she was silent since she had not made an entry of any and was a bit puzzled at the request. She was then asked about her personal rings which were removed from her during the time of her arrest. Then , they asked the question of whether she had healed the sick by wearing the rings. It was again, Joan was puzzled but did not believe it since she had never employed them in such a manner. The questioners were actually looking for evidence of talismans that were evil like those employed by witches. The questioner also asked what magical properties associated with Mandrake "Mandragora" (mandrake). The presenters were trying to connect her with the usage of magic herbs witches make use of. Joan was a bit puzzled by this because she was clueless about was the "Mandragora" plants were, and was unsure of what it was to relate to the issues that were which were being discussed at the trial. Another set of questions were posed that dealt with the issue of whether St. Michael had long or short hair, and the possibility that he was carrying an item of scales on the other. She did not answer these questions in any way.

The Verdict

The judges sat in a private sessions. The most innocuous of words she spoke were taken to mean they believed she was "false prophet,"" "a Sorcerer" as well as a witch practicing"the "magical practices." Although Joan admitted to the court that she was unaware of "Mandragora" or the "Mandragora" plant and did not make use of her rings to heal however, she was nonetheless found guilty of using these objects for evil purposes which was documented in the official record at the time of trial. In addition, she was found guilty of joining with evil spirits, and even threatening the death penalty to those who did not follow her. False accounts were also documented, and included on one the claim that she admitted she had received letters from Jesus Mary and Jesus! Mary!

The court sentenced her to burn to the ground for the ecclesiastical offence of heresy.
and Death. and Death

On the 30th day of May 1431, the priest walked into the cell of her and said:
"I am here to prepare you to die."
When she inquired about what kind of death she could encounter, he said that

she would die by fire. Joan was in a state of shock. She cried out and ran around her cell, frenzied.

"It is cruel to treat me like this! My body, which has never been harmed to be eaten today and then an ash heap?"

A cart was pulled towards the prison. Joan was wearing a white dress put on and caps that read:

"HERETIC, RELAPSED, APOSTATE, IDOLATER"

On the streets there were thousands gathering and fell to their knees as the cart passed along. They sang prayers and women were crying. After she was removed off the wagon, a pastor preached a sermon , and justified the Church's verdict by declaring that when an individual in the Church develops a disease - they should be destroyed before they cause harm to others.

She was taken to the stake, where she was secured to it. She then requested the cross she could kiss. There was no cross available however an Englishman who felt sorry for her, cut the stick into two pieces and tied it as an eagle. Then he placed it on her lips then she kissed him passionately.

Cardinal Peter Cauchon attended in the room to watch the execution. The bishop was required request prisoners to confess their guilt. He shouted his opinion loudly in front of crowds.
"I am here, Joan, to exhort you to be the last time to repent , and ask forgiveness from God."
Joan was adamant about the Divine God as the primary reason for her actions. She didn't change any of her assertions. She instead said,
"I will die because of you."

The bold assertion regarding his involvement in the matter was made clear in those words.

Then Joan was looking up to heaven and cried out a single word:
"Jesus!"

As they ignited the flame, the dark smoke instantly enveloped her body, and she was unable to see or be seen. The flames, which were orange and red, flew up and covered her beautiful and delicate body. The crowd gasped as the flames took over the entire body inflicting her with intense heat, pain and death. Horror and shock echoed through the crowd. Even the judges and witnesses who believed that she should be imprisoned were overwhelmed by guilt that she was responsible for such a horrific crime. They could not bear to listen to the constant roar of the flame. They shivered to realize they were at an unfathomable level. They were required to keep their sanity. Every muscle of their bodies wanted to twist and escape from this gruesome scene. The scene was as if it was Hell which they created for themselves to bring justice to God who was their god. The smells and the sounds of that incident affected them throughout their lives. Through the years that followed their minds were filled with monologues that justified their actions and they tried to blame the entire world other than themselves for their actions. The sentence was delivered by a group of clergymen who had lost their minds and realized that they allowed the sacredness of life to be manipulated by the slickness of political machinations.

Joan of Arc's Predictions

In some follow-up meetings at her trial Joan of Arc uttered a prediction to Cauchon. She stated,

"I advise you, before seven years, a catastrophe will strike the English and the English, many times more than the collapse in Orleans."

It was true. Charles VII returned to Paris and regained control over the city in 1436.

She spoke to bishops and clerics in her trial, and while she rattled her chains, she declared that the English lost all rights in France with the exception of cities like Calais. She stated,
"I offer you nearly 20 years to finish it."
This prediction was also realized. After Paris was taken back in 1436 by French in 1436 The French took the English out castle by castle, and town after town. In 1453 it was 1453 and the English had been completely removed from France. It was also the conclusion of the Hundred Year War.

Chapter 7: The Exoneration Of John Of Arc

"Act to act, and God will take action."
JAN OF ARC

After Joan of Arc's trial Many people fought to push for a re-examination the trial that led this woman to a brutal execution. The cause was led by Joan of the Arc's mother, Isabelle, and her brothers, Jean and Pierre. Her father had passed away in 1440 and her other siblings were dead. Her father was dead. French King Charles VII was one of the many who wanted to see that completed. In the end, Joan of Arc restored Charles VII to the rightful place as a king. He didn't make any effort to hinder her trial, whether through anger, fear or jealousy. Another reason that hindered a retrial was fact that England retained control over Rouen in 1431 , and that the Rouen had records from the trial. Charles was, no doubt, feeling guilty , and eventually had to confront the possibility that his name was going to be etched in the history of his time as Joan of Arc.

The University of Paris played a role in the trial , and could be held accountable for some of the decisions that were taken against her as they played a key role in the recruitment of Jean Beaupere, particularly as prosecutor.

in 1450. Charles VII then came out in public to restore the fame that was Joan of Arc. In order to achieve this Charles VII contacted Guillaume Bouille, a respected theologian from the University. Theologians as well as Church physicians were worried about their image. In the past both politics and religion were closely linked to the success of one's academic as well as social standing. Therefore, Bouille had to promise that they would have limited immunity. This meant that questions could be limited to questions of procedure.

The witnesses they planned to speak with, particularly Beaupere, were not cooperative because they were worried over losing their position.
Retrial Delay

In the year this retrial took place 1450, in 1450, the English were still in a few regions of France. Charles VII was then forced to shift his focus to the battlefields and reenergize his army. The English were close to leaving France completely and it was the crucial moment to get them out of the country.

In 1450, in the spring The King's army under the direction under the leadership of Jean de Clermont and Arthur de Richemont beat the English at Formigny within the Southeastern Province that bordered Spain. In 1453, the English retained certain parts of Normandy however, it was the only part of France they controlled. In Gascony near the city in Castillon, French and English forces fought each other. The legendary general Lord John Talbot, was back. He was the powerful English commander whom Joan of Arc had defeated during battles of the Loire Valley, but he had also won victories elsewhere. At the time, however, Talbot was most likely in his 60s.

At Castillon In Castillon, the English were attacked with French artillery. Despite the losses the reinforcements continued to arrive but they were not able to overcome the same challenge. Instead of acknowledging that they were defeated and surrendering, Talbot insisted that his army of exhausted soldiers continue to fight. It was a foolish decision that was more a result of pride than common wisdom. Due to his recklessness, Talbot was killed. In the Hundred Year War, it was ended.

Then the Charles was king. Charles became involved in an uprising against the feudal system and the hostility of his son Louis who was the heir apparent of the royal throne. This led him to put back attempts to discredit his wife, the Maid in Orleans. Furthermore to that, it was reported that the Catholic Church was involved in efforts to plan the Crusade to drive out the Muslims in The Holy Land in the Levant which is the region that runs in the Eastern Mediterranean Sea.

In the between, Joan of Arc's mother was determined to get Joan's release. She was determined to persuade to the French prelates to contact the pope who was to be the new Pope the Callixtus III. Callixtus III.

A lot of the French Church also wanted to restore the image of the Church, as there were those who claimed they believed that Charles VII won victory

over the English due to the intervention of an "heretic and an sorceress."
The trial of Joan of Arc 1455-1456

In response to the personal wishes from the King Charles VII, the retrial was conducted. John II Alencon and Count du Dunois were asked to provide written evidence as to the nature of Joan of Arc. Jean de Metz and Bertrand de Poulengy, the first knights who met in the palace that belonged to Duke de Beaudricourt were also required to hand in writing documents regarding the events that surrounded Joan of Arc. Unfortunately, Baudricourt had died before the retrial began which meant he could not be summoned. Bishop Peter Cauchon has since passed away, however, his children were asked to hand in their statements.

A large portion of the evidence documented within the Archives of France today was factual and described the events in this manner. This was a

method to avoid making judgments and appears to be a tactic of denial. There were, however, relevant witnesses in the second trial, such as witnesses who had been present at the trial in the first place, as well as evidence by her mother. friends from childhood and neighbors:
Isabelle Remee, Joan's mother

The record records her having stated,
"She did not think, speak or did anything against her faith...enemies were able to have her tried in the religious court. Despite her protests and denials in both written and unspoken and without any assistance in her defense she was subjected to an inhumane, violent, and sinning trial. Judges falsely condemned her legally and in the most gruesome manner and sentenced her to death by burning. In order to slay their souls and to pay for the infamous, shameful and irreparable loss for me and my family. I ask that her name be reinstated."

Father Martin Ladvenu, a Dominican priest from Rouen

Ladvenu's testimony revealed that Ladvenu stated that a lot of were present at the trial.

"did more because of the affection for"the English and the respect they received rather than because of a genuine passion for justice and the Catholic belief."

In relation to his personal testimony in his trial for Joan of Arc, he regretted that he behaved himself in an unprofessional and an exemplary manner during her trial.

The Bishop Jean Massieu, the notary during Joan of Arc's trial. Joan of Arc

Massieu said that a lot witnesses spoke to him privately and tried to convince him to alter the statements that Joan was able to say during her trial. This is today referred to as manipulating the evidence and is considered a crime in the majority of countries in Europe. Regarding his own views He also stated that he was a fan of Joan of Arc and believed the assertions she made in relation regarding her dreams.

Bishop Jean Beaupere, the prelate who was prosecutor

He never changed or deviated from his convictions that Joan was deluded and her dreams weren't real but merely fictionalized. He believed that Joan of Arc a wily and devious woman.

Jean Waterin, laborer and her former childhood friend of Joan

Jean was a witness about Joan's early time at Domremy and said that at times his fellow children and I would make fun of her. He believed that she was actually religious and would sometimes go to a chapel in order to "talk to God." If she heard church bells sound the time to pray at midday, she stated that she would kneel in reverence.

Dominique Jacob, priest of Joan's village church

He said in court that Joan of Arc was very religious and well-behaved when she was an infant. He also mentioned that she always kneeled at the sound of the bells of the Angelus during the midday hours and was a regular worshiper.

Concluding Statements

In 1456 In his brief, Jean Brehal, the Grand Inquisitor in this trial wrote:
"We declare that in certain areas it is true that her testimony have been ignored in silence. On other issues her confessions have been misinterpreted. We assert that certain words have been changed in a way to alter their substance."

With that and other statements that were included in the ecclesiastical record The Inquisitor concluded the verdicts of the Court of Inquisition in Joan of Arc's case was faked and misinterpreted. Brehal's statement completely discredited Joan of Arc and placed all the blame on those who were biased judges. This meant that the entire process that had initially was adamant about Joan of Arc was nullified.

Peter Cauchon, who led the trial of Joan of Arc, was posthumously branded a heretic. Following his trial for Joan of Arc, Peter Cauchon lived a quiet life and passed away from heart failure in 1442. He was buried at the cathedral of Rouen however, according to one story - the body was later disinterred and dumped into the city's sewers.

However in the case of Joan there are no physical remains. The tower of her stone prison in Rouen is still standing as a evidence of some of the more scandalous incidents of French history.

Chapter 8: The Maid

Jehanne D'Arc was born in 1412 in the town in Domremy, France, the daughter of tenant farmers Jacques d'Arc and his wife, Isabelle Romee. The exact date of her birth is not known however the most common belief stems from a letter written in 1429 from a certain Perceval de Boullainvillers that mentions her birth on the date that was Epiphany (celebrated in the church of Christians on the 6th of January) of 1412.

As her birthday might suggest that, for an individual with a well recorded later life There are plenty that are missing in the understanding of Joan. Even her name carries complexities. Her name is often referred to as"the Anglicized "Joan of Arc" after her father Jacques Surname. However, that doesn't necessarily indicate that the family was out of "Arc," and Jacques could have been referred to in other ways (e.g "Jacob d'Arc," "Jaqe d'Arc," "Jacques Tarc" or "Darc"). Joan may have been identified as "Jehanne

Romee,"" because in her home town the girls were given their mother's name. But "Romee" as name was not easy to use in indicating parental lineage. It was often applied to those who had made a journey of pilgrimage, either to Rome or another sacred site. In short, the medieval France wasn't governed to strict and rigid rules about surnames.

The father of Joan, Jacques carried some cachet as a comparatively prosperous farmer in their tiny village. The family was not rich, however, and Joan lived a relatively simple household life. She was not taught writing or reading, but her devoted mother steered her to the doctrines that were taught by The Catholic Church. Joan was a determined but holy girl who looked after their animals, harvested the harvest, and was known as a skilled seamstress and spinner.

At 13 years of age at the age of 13, she began to experience dreams and heard voices coming from Catholic characters.

In the course of her later trial she told of the first time she heard voices she was in the garden of her family and noticed a bright, glowing light and sound coming "from towards the Church." Church bells ringing often greeted the voices. Similar experiences would happen to her repeatedly throughout her existence. She recalled encounters with the warrior saint, St. Michael the Archangel and the brave martyrs of virgins, St. Catherine of Alexandra and St. Margaret of Antioch.

What message do they have for the humble peasant girl?

Her task was to complete the noble task of ridding France completely of English presence and crowning her the French dauphin Charles VII, its legitimate King.

The Hundred Years The Hundred Years Joan was a turbulent time for her nation. At the time she was born, France was already entangled in war with England during what was known as "The Hundred Year's War" between 1337 and 1453. The primary issue was legitimate succession to the French throne when Charles IV of France died in 1328 without having a son. The throne was inherited by his cousin, and his former count of Valois, the king Philip VI. Edward III of England, however, also made the claim that a corner contests were more legitimate and he was Charles IV's most close male kin as the mother of his father is Charles the IV's sister. In addition there was a time when in Medieval Europe the kings were able to acquire titles outside of their own kingdoms. So, at the moment of Charles IV's demise, Edward III of England with his titles of the Count of Ponthieu and Duke of Guyenne (which was located in Aquitaine on French land) was also his vassal.

Philip VI succeeded his cousin Charles IV with the help of an French assembly that was for a while believed to be a good idea for Edward III. However, Philip VI's seizure of Guyenne's duchy in 1337 Guyenne in England during 1337 deemed to be provocative enough to trigger an increase in tensions. Edward III pursued his claim to the French throne, and began the war by sending an army sent to Flanders and thus launching an ongoing conflict that would go for more than a 100 years... But not that the two nations had any affection for one another in the early days. What transpired in 1337 are the climax of a longer-lasting, intermittent war between the two countries which some scholars trace all the way back to Norman Conquest of 1066, and some even put it that it didn't really end at all until when the Entente Cordiale of 1904. If one agrees or disagrees to this view it is crucial to remember is that the weight of war is very heavy across France and England and that famous French political figure Charles de Gaulle could go further and say that - in the year 1962 - that France's "greatest hereditary foe" was the British, more so than Germany.

The Hundred Year's War proved bloody on a variety of different levels in French as well as English life There were the characteristics that resembled "total conflict" in the manner in which the battles were executed. The notion that of "total war" was not articulated and scrutinized until more modern times (beginning with the military theorist Carl von Claasewitz's work during the late 19th century) however, the events that took place in France during the 14th century seemed be in line with the traits of a non-stop strategy for achieving the victory. The tax-paying French peasantry, as an example were terribly affected by raids dubbed "Chevauchee" even though they weren't combatants. As crucial sources of income which eventually financed military pursuits and wars, they were seen by the English monarchy's "The The Black Prince" Edward, for example as logical target. Apart from the economic motives they were also targeted to discredit and denigrate their leaders, and also to provide the raiding soldiers the opportunity to earn money.

When Edward was executing his "grande the chevauchee" of the early 1350s for instance estimates at the time pointed to the destruction of 18,000 square miles on French territory. The conflict between these two nations, therefore, was long-running, deep-seated and did not just affect the military field or certain segments of society. It was present in the daily lives of the majority of people.

At Joan's own home village of Domremy as an example there were numerous confrontations with soldiers from the Hundred Years of War. The church in the village was burned at one time and Joan was required to lead the family's livestock away from the violence several times.

One of the most significant battles in the beginning stages of the Hundred Year's War was the Battle of Crecy in northern France 1346, which was a disastrous loss for the French despite their greater numbers; and The Battle of Poitiers in 1356 and 1356. Edward III of England's son, Edward the Black Prince had succeeded in capture of the French King, John II (son of Philip VI, who was killed in 1350) in 1356; and also thirteen years later, in the Battle of Agincourt of 1415 which was the 1415 Battle of Agincourt, an English win immortalized in William Shakespeare in his play, Henry V (which contains one of the most exuberant lines in literature ever written, "We few, we happy few, we are a band of brothers. For the one today who sheds blood alongside me will become my brother ...").

In essence the war continued to the point that the primary protagonists were dead before they were even near to being over, and the countries that were involved were forced to fight an international conflict in addition to numerous of internal conflicts.

The three wars mentioned above in particular the first was a victory for Edward III of England's time however, the second one was a victory against a

France that was under the original opponent's son John II. John II passed away during captivity as did his son Charles V of France was to be the one to carry on the conflict. Charles V's child, Charles VI, however, had mental problems that brought about a different succession problem within France. This ultimately led to a civil war between Armagnacs as well as Burgundians. This internal conflict was among the main reasons that the King Henry V of England, profiting from the French conflict, re-established his English right to claim an heir to the French throne. It's not to say that the English monarchy was not amidst significant upheavals of its own during the duration of the Hundred Year of War. Henry V, after all was the result of his father Henry IV's dethronement the successor to Edward III Richard II.

This was then the world in which a small French peasant girl, named Joan was able to enter. There was a long-running war among the French with the English.

It was an unpopular war with "national" in its vast impact on a vast majority of the population. There was conflict in the absence of and also within the midst of a France divided by internal conflict. There was internal conflict. English monarch Henry V even had Frenchmen who sided with him - he formed allies with Burgundians in the reign of Philip the Good, the Duke of Burgundy. Henry V's victories in the military as well as his victory in the Armagnac murder of Philip the Good's father, John, reportedly motivated the Burgundians to join the English.

An alliance formed between English King and French Burgundians resulted in the Treaty of Troyes in 1420. In the terms of the treaty, Henry V would become the mad French King Charles VI's heir and disinherited his daughter, Charles of Valois (later, Charles VII). Henry V, who would marry Charles VI's daughter Catherine was to be Charles VI's regent when he was in his life and after his death Henry V would claim the French throne. He would then become The King of the "double sovereigns" that included England in addition to France.

It is worth noting that the battles mentioned earlier in the Hundred Years of War resulted in victories for England and often against adversity odds. The 1420 treaty also allowed the English a firm hold over French interests. In fact, at times the ultimate winners in the Hundred Year's War the French were seen to be in the losing side.

This would change when a young peasant girl who claimed to listen to the voice of Saints who were giving her a divine task appeared in the scene.

Chapter 9: War Hero

What could a seemingly unimportant tiny French young woman in the nation, barely in her adulthood, uninitiated possibly adrift and female in the time when women's duties were severely restricted can contribute to the long-running war that was fought by a rotating group of powerful princes and monarchs? What can anyone expect of Jehanne D'Arc from Domremy as there were two great powers in the world and more than 100 years of diplomatic and military experience had already been brought be used by powerful men in a war that seemed to have no definitive conclusion?

This was due to her charisma, or perhaps divinely-given wisdom of authority and knowledge (if one believed in the aforementioned convictions) which enabled her to be in a position to overcome her past and make her way to the courts of Dauphin Charles and then to the battlefields with huge assets, and finally into an the unforgettable victory that enthralled the capital city, Orleans.

Road to Orleans

Joan of Arc had a many obstacles to overcome before she was able to travel towards the place that would later make her legend, and later became a national icon and saint. One of these was the expectations she was placed upon her as an era-defining woman. At the age of 16 of age, family members tried to get for Joan an unplanned wedding. But she had already taken an oath of chastity regard to her divine calling which had up to this point been a constant presence in her thoughts and heart for a long time. Joan was even required to appear before an local court in order to convince officials to release her from the game. It was believed that virginity was the most prized attribute in that society, possibly greater than marriage. The woman had even taken to calling herself Jehanne la Pucelle or "Joan as the Maid," with the "maid" as a sign of the purity of her character. Whatever way, having been being free of a marriage she was not interested in she was capable of pursuing her chosen task.

Guiding Voices. The divine purpose that captivated the woman was one which would gradually be revealed to her and she would be coached and guided through three holy voices. They were Saint. Michael the Archangel; Saint Catherine of Alexandria and Saint Margaret of Antioch. Additionally, there had also been a mention of her encounters as a Saint Gabriel. It is essential to comprehend the significance of her three primary saintly influences due to their significance to the progression that Joan of Arc's journey.

Saint Michael became the first saint to be able to communicate with Joan in the age of just thirteen years old. She was required to visit several times before recognizing the person he was. Archangel Michael is the protector saint for law enforcers personnel and soldiers.

He is frequently depicted in armor and wings, as well as an arm drawn with a strong stance over an serpent. There is a military connection in Joan's story, however saint Michael is also the patron of France's royal house at that time, in addition to being a well-known woman's champion due to being a protector of Mother Mary - which are all relevant to Joan of Arc's unique circumstances.

The saints Catherine from Alexandria along with Margaret from Antioch (who may also referred to as Marina) served as the protectors and counsellors of Joan as well. Their stories ended up sharing remarkable similarities. Saint Margaret was the daughter of a pagan priest changed her religion to Christianity and bowed her life to God. She resisted the proposal to marry the prefect, who later was sent to prison, been tortured, and was subjected to a trial in public. She was executed with a being beheaded. Saint Catherine was a noblewoman who lived in Alexandria who changed her religion to Christianity as well and shrewdly criticized her Emperor's repression of the religion. She was offered a favorable marriage, in which she could renounce her Christianity and, as Saint Margaret was also taken a vow to abstinence. She was imprisoned and her faith was repeatedly tested but she stood and defend her beliefs in such a manner that conversions were swiftly followed after her. Saint Catherine was tortured, and eventually executed. As with the saints mentioned above, Joan of Arc was an innocent martyr who had to fight against authorities for her convictions. In the course in her life her faith was repeatedly challenged , and it was and she would be a person of enthusiasm and awe. She was a lot similar to another saint Catherine and, indeed many of the people from her day had said that she was like a saint.

The saint Saint Michael who advised Joan she would also receive advice from Saints

Catherine along with Margaret. In the following three years in her existence, these saints guided her in preparations for a job she was unable to comprehend until she was 17. Before then her goals were to be a kid to God as well as a virgin who lived an exemplary life that was lived according to His instructions. When she was 17 years old, the saintly Saint Michael began to be a more frequent visitor and eventually explained to Joan her motives for freedom of her nation. Joan initially doubted her abilities as being a "poor girl who had no knowledge about war and riding," but she eventually realized that when God was directing her to leave to war, then she had to go. With the assistance of these voices, whom she considered to be her protectors She was given confidence, strength and direction - and sometimes, even warnings of danger that helped her during her first-ever campaign.

In 1428, the village situated in Domremy had been attacked with English or

Burgundian forces, forcing her family to leave until it was again safe. In other words she didn't go away from home and in the end the next (and final) time she left she was in pursuit the purpose of life. She wanted to get access to the man whom she felt obliged to crown as The King of France. The geography and her position however, combined to keep her from meeting the Dauphin.

Charles was the ruler of France to the south of Loire River; Domremy was located to the east. While a lot of the area of Joan's home was still committed to Charles but the territories around it weren't always so as some areas held an alliance with the Duchy of England, which was allied with Burgundy. It would not be an easy task even if she managed to convince anyone of her story and get her to Chinon, where Charles was the throne of Chinon.

Her journey began on the instructions of Michael's voice. Michael. She left Domremy towards the town of Burey-le-

Petit in which a close friend, Durand Lassois resided. She informed him of her task over a span for several days, and he was impressed in by the determination of her, accompanied her to Vaucouleurs which is a village inhabited by the loyalists of daphin Charles. She contacted an official in the area, known as Sir Robert de Baudricourt. She explained her intention to meet with Charles at Chinon to convince the dauphin about her purpose, and she required Sir Robert's help and resources to reach her goal. His response varied between laughing dismissing her to that what she needed was to get was "a good kiss" and that she should be sent home to the father. In any case, he handed her a string of rejections. However, Joan was unstoppable and had a trick up her sleeves - an prophecy. She informed Sir Robert of a particular French victory in the military (later to be called The Battle of Herring) that would then be revealed by the messenger. Additionally, she was winning over people. The Sir Robert de Baudricourt was soon attracted by Joan's desire to meet the dauphin and he was reported to have provided Joan with a sword horse and an entourage made up of three knights, a squire, and four other men. In order to protect her, Joan had to travel from Vaucouleurs with her hair cut short and dressed as the man she was.

They travelled a smooth 150 miles in just 11 days through unrestricted territory and eventually arrived at Chinon in the Chinon region, in which Joan wrote to Charles to ask for an audience. The dauphin was in need of convincing. He talked to his counsellors and the church members to decide whether she was worthy of his attention according to our past, he ultimately accepted... however, not with a second test. Charles famously changed his clothes using an alternative and mingled with the large crowd of courtiers who were interested to meet the young woman who claimed to be a gift from God. Joan did not disappoint.

She famously recognized him immediately thanks to her voices that always been her guide. She told him about her mission to liberate France of the English and included his oath as The King of France.

The Anointing of an French King

Charles, the Dauphin, Charles, was in many ways already a king at the time Joan of Arc was seeking for him at Chinon around 1429. The day his father Charles VI passed away in 1422, according to some historians they believed that he was already a King, despite not having any formal coronation. This sense of humour can be summarized with the phrase, "The King is dead. The King lives on!" Even prior to the death of his father He was already serving as regent. Many, however, believe that coronation confers a spiritual legitimacy on the monarch. In this sense it is believed that crowning recognizes the absolute power of God and that the anointing ceremony is comparable to binding the monarch to uphold the law, religion and security of his citizens. According to this perspective the coronation ceremony has important.

The time of France during the reign of Joan of Arc, being the King was not as easy and the dauphin. According to tradition, the coronation ceremony of French Kings took place in Reims, the Cathedral of Reims, which has a long tradition of anointing the nation's top leaders. It is believed that the Merovingian King Clovis I., who played a important figure in the creation of France was baptized at Reims in the 498-499 years of holy oil. This gave the place authority in the anointing ceremony of the nation's rulers, but it took some time to become the standard place of coronation for French monarchs during the eleventh century. Then, from 1027-1825 there were a total of 29 French Kings were coronated at Reims.

Charles VII was almost not one of them.

It was his father's name. King Edward VII However, he was not the most senior. The older brother of his died in 1417 when he reached fourteen years old, making him the successor to the throne. He was born during the same turbulent period when he was Joan of Arc, and as the dauphin of a conflicting Kingdom, his life was particularly at risk. When his country's capital city in 1418 he was forced to leave south. The year was also when in which he was appointed the role as regent for his deranged dad, Charles VI. After his father's death in 1422, October, he was declared the de facto monarch of France. He faced a number of challenges - budgetary problems as well as failed reconciliation attempts with the Burgundians as well as those of the English as well as its French allies gained ground. His adversaries held the north, including Reims. He was reported to be depressed and perhaps was thinking of surrendering to the pressure imposed by English forces and settling for an unhurried retirement far from the rat race. At this point an old lady with a message arrived with a lot of force upon his doorstep. She was convinced that she was able to aid her country and also her dauphin. She planned to have his crown by Reims' Cathedral located in Reims.

Reversing the Siege of Orleans

Henry V of England passed in 1422 prior to that insane Charles VI of France whom was to succeed to Henry V of England under the Treaty of Troyes. Charles VI passed away just two months later in the following year. Henry V and Catherine's son, Henry VI of England was, as a result, Henry VI, the King of the "double monarchy" not his father, who was the main force behind England's victories in war against the French and had signed the 1420 treaty. The teen Henry VI, who was just aged nIne months was a northern France which included Paris. However, down south, with the 'Dauphinists the Armagnacs continued to support the cause of Late French the King

Charles VI's oldest son, the crown prince Charles of Valois.

In the midst of Henry VI still so young His cousin, John the Duke of Bedford was appointed to the role of a regent. The goal of his reign was to consolidate those English forces in northerly areas, to move southwards. The most important element in an offensive in the southern part was the strategically important city of Orleans that remained in loyal relationship with its Dauphin, Charles VII. The English began their assault on October 14, 1428. It was , in many ways the beginning of the end for English claim to France.

In the early 1429s, Joan of Arc was presented to the court by dauphin Charles and was able discern him from the multitude of faces. To strengthen her standing she also presented him with the sign of God which only the King was capable of recognizing. She could have been echoing the prayer that the dauphin said to God. Whatever the meaning of this gesture and it is still unknown however, it was enough to convince Charles to believe in her even though the latter was not able to trust her at once or fully. He took her to a few theologians and church leaders coming from Chinon and the University of Poitiers for weeks of interrogation and examination. In the end, these reputable experts found that Joan was genuine, pure and humility as well as theological piety. This is enough to be a resounding endorsement to convince Charles to let her join his army, armed with substantial assets.

Joan of Arc was made the official commander of a group comprised of veteran commanders, who led around 10,000-12,000 soldiers. Based on her goals they had to go towards Orleans to break the lengthy English siege that was raging there. She was a young, inexperienced girl, surrounded by experienced warriors, but she was soon able to demonstrate the ability to fight and a leadership style that went that was beyond her age and gender, which would make a man fall in love with. In a way her limitations were severe, which gave her role more credibility and weight, because what else could "the Maid" be able to develop her skills apart from the voices of God which have guided her throughout her life?

Additionally, even though it might seem a bit absurd today what would motivate anyone to offer an untried female a chance to lead an army? There are logical reasons to believe that in Medieval Europe such a woman as Joan of Arc would have had the ability to command as much power as she could have for her divine task.

Medieval Teenage Warriors. Firstof all, her young age may be not been quite as big an obstacle to serving in the military as it may appear on first sight. The information on the average age of soldiers during the time is scarce as there isn't sufficient reliable writing documents or authentic excavations of medieval remains. What is certain is that, regardless of whether young people made up a significant proportion of the fighting force in Medieval Europe, there is no doubt that they existed in the battlefields during the period.

"The Children's Crusade" - A popular religious movement that was sweeping across Europe during the 13th century, and was dominated by youngsters. It was short-livedand not sanctioned by the religious authorities, and thus, not one of the members has been believed to have fulfilled his objectives of reaching out to the Holy Land; and its history as the result of a "youth movement" is" is disputed. However, young people were a prominent members of"the "Crusaders," and this is evident in the surviving documents from the time. In the Hundred Year's War, one the most famous of its characters, England's "Black Prince" Edward, began his legend at his first day at the Battle of Crecy at the age of 16. He was a man of high risk in the vanguard. His King's father advised that the prince should be given the chance of "win the battle of his spurs." It was a victory for the English.

It is the Power of Religion. This is why Joan of Arc's youthful age, though probably more of an exception rather than the norm for medieval soldiers, nevertheless did not stop her from taking part in the battle. The position she held as a leader, however was unusual. Edward "The Black Prince" was expected by his position in the role of English Prince's son by the King to possess an enviable military status and also an image of bravery and strength He was also educated in that manner. Joan of Arc did not possess that background. We can see the strength of her religious background. In the past the argument of religion for leadership was compelling. the wars and their outcomes were heavily infused with religious beliefs, which were sometimes viewed as an indication of divine judgment. In this context her leadership as a titular leader of an army is to be a reasonable expectation for a religious leader who was able to demonstrate her authenticity. She was not the first neither was she the last. Joan of Arc was just special in that she was able to perform her title of leader in a pivotal moment of the Hundred Years of War.

The changing Role for Women. Medieval Europe was certainly an era of patriarchy with distinct gender roles for both women and men. In actual the underlying issue of the Hundred Years war was a gendered question - could the reign of France be passed on to women or via women? The war's beginning point, actually was the demise of Charles IV who had no sons but had infant daughters. French authorities omitted the girls, and then crowned an ancestor traced to the male lineage, Philip VI. Another one was overlooked were one of the heirs to English the King Edward III, who would have had a greater claim to his mother. Therefore, the answer was a clear "No" on the issue of female heirs. This speaks volumes about the low status of women in the society of the time.

This is in line with the common belief that women were delegated to subordinate and/or domestic or minor duties in the medieval age. However, they were an integral element of society, possessing enormous authority and power across the vastest areas to the centres of power. The reason for this is a variety of reasons.

The war of 100 years led to the fact that soldiers, no matter if they were warlords or commanders or a large number of soldiers, had to leave a lot of matters at home in the hands of women when they travelled to battle. This included financial, manual and administrative work. Women were often found working in fields that are traditionally associated with males such as forging armour and weaponry. Some absences were temporary, when they were caused through war - the aforementioned injuries, captures and death - absences were more long-lasting and women needed to adapt in line with. In addition to the war, illness was also part in the increasing importance of women. Certain diseases, such as that of Black Death, reportedly claimed more children and adults than women. Additionally, during a period of princes and Kings and their infirm leaders in their twenties, fighting or wounded or sick or even mad (as many monarchs were as well, with spells even in the reign of Charles VI) was a sign of increased responsibilities for wife and their mothers (sometimes and sometimes, their powerful lovers). This was on top of the roles women in the upper echelons of society have had in the form of brokering alliances through matchmaking and marriage, the wise management of their royal children, strengthening their relationships and improving the image of their husbands by using "soft power"" and negotiating with the sovereign in support of diverse causes. At times, women were deployed into battle. combat in roles that were similar to the ones assigned to Joan as spiritual visionaries, or as symbolic Aristocrats who represented their husbands, fathers or sons. Sometimes, they were sent into the middle of the battle. Jeanne De Montfort, Duchess of Brittany, (1310-1376) repelled French attacks on the estate of her husband, which was a hotly contested one after being imprisoned and captured. Another noblewoman from the in the period, this one in Scotland, Agnes Dunbar (1312-1369) was a hero for her fight to defend her husband's fortress from her fellow English in the time of Edward III. It was not just the English who were a threat to their fortress. French were also home to a female heroine in Julienne de Guesclin (1333-1405) and an Abbess. In fact, there was a strong female character within the court of dauphin Charles of Valois and his mother-in-law Yolande of Aragorn was admired for her shrewd mind and ability to negotiate and her financial acumen. She was a pioneering advocate in the cause of Joan of Arc, recognizing quickly that the young visionary of religion could be a key player in their cause.

That's how a teenager untrained, not-so-experienced girl ended up in a position that allowed her to make significant changes in the midst of an unending conflict. Her age and gender were unusual, however, they were not uncommon and her faith was an argument that was compelling for times. It may also be one of the reasons why the dauphin was wary, known as undecisive and inactive and running out of options. Her temperament probably played in the mix as well. It was reported that she was quite charismatic and spoke with authority. Indeed, she attracted a lot of believers and admirers even prior to her legendary turn at Orleans.

Additionally, during the time of her campaign, she demonstrated astonishingly and, according to some, miraculously inspiring, abilities for combat that would boost her role on the battlefield beyond her role as a mere persona. Her bravery and determination at last captivated the attention of veterans and captivated the attention of many men, encouraging even those who had been reluctant to stand with Charles VII in the fight against the Anglo-Burgundian alliance.

A stopover in Blois as well as Checy. Before departing for Orleans the city, it is believed to have stopped in Blois, a town in Blois near to the battle. According to historians they say that she met her troops there, and then she primarily concentrated on repairing the spiritual aspects of camp. The usual mix of prostitution, alcohol and relationships, gambling, and swearing that seemed be a common theme among the fighting forces of the world regardless of the location or time of the year. However, Joan of Arc would have none of it. She was said to have demanded the marriage of unwed lovers, removal of lovers, as well as regular Mass and confessions among the soldiers. She prohibited civilians from looting and stopped swearing. It was an enormous task for a diverse army that comprised nobles, veteran soldiers and mercenaries. But most of them were able to comply.

Her reputation was that she was generally sweet and quiet and a fan of staying in her own space at least until she was confronted by an offense to God which she was later to confront with what would eventually become a well-known temperament. She preferred to be alone however, she would occasionally be with her aristocratic commanders or with a clergy group. She was gorgeous and slender even in the uniform of a soldier she wore to blend in. Her men would say she was not subject to their desires. Some would go as that they were not compelled to sin at her side. Yet, one of her ritual was to lay down in complete armor, in order to guard her purity.

They set off from Blois and, three days later, she was greeted by Jean Dunois, Lord Dunois the 26-year-old commander who was defending Orleans. Dunois was popularly known for his role as "le Batard d'Orleans" (it is not a reference to his character or the way his conduct was during the battle, but a very frank reference to his family and the circumstances surrounding being born to the lover of an eminent nobleman). They had a meeting at Checy just across the river from the place she wanted to be - which quite fitting for the fiery girl, exactly where there the English were. Dunois faced the full strength of her character because she was not happy with the decision that was made to protect her, especially due to the wind's unfavorable conditions which was causing her barges from her army difficulties crossing. Her speech contained a criticism about how God's guidance was "safer and more sensible" than those who believed that she should go to Checy was an excellent idea. Many witnesses have confirmed that her speech signaled an immediate change in winds, which would allow for a limited crossing in her army. Others would need to wait for her.

Arrival at Orleans. Joan arrived in Orleans at the end of April, 1429. day of April 1429. At this point, Orleans was already in the hands of the English for a number of months, beginning in the month of October preceding year. The English strategy was to strike with a modest force that, though not able to conduct a swift and decisive siege, could suffice to famine the garrison. It appeared to be working. It seemed to be an easy way to break the tightening noose of the English. Then came that important date in April. Joan is believed to have walked under the darkness at night at the eastern gate of the city, as the French team diverted the opposing English on the west side. The reason she arrived late could be due to fears regarding the English or to stop her from being surrounded by people who were who were eager to meet her who had heard about their hero's imminent arrival. The crowds were large crowds of people who were enthralled, pressing against one another for an ointment or her white horse that she taken on. According to some accounts she appeared like an angel from God.

She was awe-inspiring by herself, but came with essential reinforcements and other supplies. This was a boost to confidence in those in the French guards in Orleans and also the likelihood of them winning. In the days prior to this,, they were a demoralized unit and many were still grieving the weight of losing during the Battle of Herrings just weeks ago, and being trapped in a city being held by English forces from three sides.

Joan was working hard to get her task cut out for her. The English had constructed a chain of fortresses, using completely new structures as well as modified one (including churches) in order to seal Orleans in. What is the best way to dismantle such an established besiege?

The battles did not begin immediately. The French side decided to hold off until they had other soldiers Joan had on her side and who were unable to get across at the same time as she did. In between she wrote a series of messages to English soldiers and asked to get out of the way. In one message, before going to going into battle, she declared, "I am sent here by God as to the King in Heaven to take your body and soul out of France ..." The messages were not considered serious, and were frequently reacted with insults by bilingual English officers who used their expertise in witty slurs against her good character and even mocked her heritage with the term "vachere" - - a girl who cares for cows. At first she was also accused of being a sorcerer. Despite this, Joan was even willing to speak in person several times in order to ask the English to be redeemed in the name of God. However, only a few rebukes and insults were the result. The English did not appear to change their mind, at the very least not at the request by "La Pucelle" which was the "Maid" who was sent by God. They would need to settle the matter in the battle field.

In the meantime, waiting for the other men to arrive, Joan was busy with the church, became familiar to the English fortifications in Orleans and then became visible to people who were who were hungry for her presence. Even escorted tours were taken around the streets. The peace would only last a few hours. The remaining reinforcements came in - slightly smaller than they were originally according to reports, with the loss of soldiers caused by Joan's absence. The English had reinforcements and supplies arriving too. Joan of Arc was going to battle shortly thereafter.

A late... but timely arrival. Joan's first encounter with fighting for Orleans was in a battle that she was actually delayed for. On May 4 she awoke up suddenly and was compelled by her guidance voices to fight with the English. What she was not aware of, but that as she was asleep, soldiers were been fighting in the vicinity of the fortified cathedral St. Loup (one of the buildings near Orleans which the English changed to meet their purposes). The church was not advised by her commanding officers or perhaps the page boy charged with the task was not doing his job in the duties he was expected to perform. In any case, she leapt into her armor and onto her horse, unfurled her banner and rushed towards the scene of battle.

The way towards St. Loup gave the young girl a terrifying glimpse of the terrible horrors of the war. There were horrific injuries to her fellow countrymen, and blind eyes of the dead. She was aching and grieving for the dead. As she arrived at St. Loup she found the French fighting, but it weren't going to last long. The sight of her energetic charge was enough to boost French attempts, but within a short time the English defenses almost collapsed. Reforcing efforts were also resisted well leaving St. Loup in the in the hands of France. They had smashed the English's long siege and everybody knew that.

Joan made a gracious victor. She called for mercy for Englishmen who were disguised (either legitimately or in disguise) as clergymen and were captured in the course of the battle. She wept and grieved for her fallen adversaries. She also urged her triumphant team to confess and express their gratitude to God. She was kind and compassionate... however she was also certain of one thing: The siege in Orleans was, she stated, was going to be broken in five days.

Five Days. Joan of Arc suspended fighting on holy days. This signified that of her prophecy and prophecy she would see the English siege would be lifted within five days, they were given much less time in comparison to. The 5th of May on it was Feast of the Ascension, there was no fight, however she did shoot an arrow towards the English and was followed by an e-mail that the English snubbed for being written by a woman.

The other side wasn't the only one who was scathing about her, though. Her image was for many considered to be a child, mad or just a woman any of the above probably inexperienced and maybe even an interloper. She was an inexperienced the title commander. However, those who didn't believe in these views may have been confused about her position within the command structure, or what they could anticipate from her, and how they could be doing with her. In any case when it came to making decisions on strategies and plans prior to and during the following days of fighting, doors and the decisions were not open for "La Pucelle" and, even if they told her about the plans, she was not informed of the entire extent of the details. This was unpopular with "La Pucelle," but she was not the "Maid," but she had her own "counseland counsel" her relationship with God that she believed will be successful.

It was true and throughout through her campaign no injury could hinder her from becoming an inspiration to the troops. The battle began on the 6th May and saw the French expanding their territory towards the most crucial fortress held by the English in the region - Les Tourelles. As the day's battles was over, the French had taken the strongholds that were heading towards it, which included the fortified Church in St. Jean-Le-Blanc and the fortified monastery of the Augustins. This was in no small measure to a daring march that was led by Joan of Arc and one of her most faithful commanders, Etienne Vignolles. He was called "La Hire" for his personal rage (he was also famous as a positive influencer on an individual who, prior to the time fighting alongside her throughout her campaigns was known for his the raunchy and vulgar speech).

The next item on the list included the Les Tourelles itself. In the course of the fight on the 7th of Mai, the actress was hit by an arrow that hit her between the shoulder and neck which was a sprain that she had anticipated and was forewarned of. The pain was grave, but she barely missed any beat. After a quick change of clothes, her back into the middle of it, and her determination was so inspirational that the English eventually gave up.

On May 8th The English were retreating, and as it was a Sunday, holy Joan chose to stay clear of the pursuit. They had retreated to Orleans as per Joan's divine plan.

It is interesting to note that the 8th of May also was an important feast day for the saint of St. Michael the Archangel.

The Battle Standard of Joan of Arc.

In the above accounts it is interesting to observe that they refer to Joan of Arc's presence in combat, but don't mention her fighting. In fact, the literature on Joan does not mention her killing anyone. She certainly was dressed in her armor and she'd be remembered the most for this raiment. She was also a force for men lift their swords, and she definitely did her part... However, she was a war hero who didn't personally combat or kill her adversaries. On the other hand, she attempted to first seek out diplomatic solutions and then, in the event of their refusal attempt to help with strategies. On the field, she was more of an uninvolved mascot with her banner was almost always in her hand.

Joan's banner was said to measure three feet by twelve feet. It was white and long and was made of a fabric that resembled canvas . It was also backed with a silk fringe. The banner was embellished with the representation of God holding the world , being surrounded by two angels and an inscription "Jhesus Maria" printed on the banner. Joan of Arc used the banner that she claimed she loved much more than swords to indicate to the direction of a rally. The white banner could be a prominent feature amid the chaos of battle. There were two additional flag-like equipments during her campaign. The triangular pennon with The Virgin Mary, the archangel Gabriel and the French kingdom's symbol of a flower was held by a squire . It was used to mark the location of her on the field. The banner also depicting the Crucifixion and the Crucifixion, which was where men came to participate in religious ceremonies in line with her pleas for the soldiers to be more religious and in accordance with her own religious practice.

A Promise to Keep at Reims

The triumph at Orleans was a major draw for all the world however the French court of Charles, the dauphin Charles did not seem fully prepared - indeed it never was to fully trust in Joan of Arc's judgment or skill, or to surrender their fates to her instructions. She had to actually push Charles to go to Reims to be crowned. She eventually succeeded in persuading Charles and his advisors as well. Joan of Arc and her followers followed Charles through hostile terrain, only engaging whenever necessary until they arrived at Reims in 1429. According to some reports, the route was one that was a "bloodless" one, it was a feat in and of itself in the event that it was true that just by her name were the towns that were occupied by English on the route under siege.

As per the stated goal of Joan of Arc, Charles VII, King of France was crowned at Reims as did many other French monarch before his time. She was on his side, a beloved banner held in her hands.

Chapter 10: The Heretic

At this time in the course of her career, Joan of Arc had demonstrated her skill in breaking through the siege at Orleans and allowing her daughter to get honored as Charles VII at the Cathedral in Reims. She was a popular figure by her fellow citizens, and was greatly admired from her King Charles VII. However, it was also the highest point of her active participation and accomplishments during the Hundred Year War.

Certain groups of the Charles VII court were believing that she was too powerful. It was also evident that her style of conduct as well as the approach from Charles VII was very different He was more prudent in his approach and was more diplomatic. Her on the other hand only wanted to get on with her task. Her insistence on advancing French efforts towards retaking Paris for instance, was unsuccessful and didn't make her popular with many. The image of her is also believed to have suffered a scuff during a battle that occurred on a sacred day such as the day of the day of the Virgin Mary's birthday on the 8th of September which also saw her injured in her thigh.

In 1430, a short time after her legendary victory against English troops at Orleans and making good on her pledge of a reward to Charles VII for his crowing at Reims the following year, she was captured by her foes during a fight with Burgundians in Compliegne. They paraded her with pride by her enemies and kept for a long time before she was ultimately transferred to English to pay the ransom of the king of around 10,000 pounds.

A trial was soon to follow. When she was employed to confer Charles VII credibility, she was considered by their adversaries as a means to defame his legitimacy. One of the charges made at her was witchcraft as well as heresy. One of the most fundamental ideas of the time was If she was a genuine messenger from God and God's messenger, then why would her experience failure and be captured? If she wasn't an agent of God and therefore, under what authority was she operating under? With these implications, Joan of Arc then began to appear more and more like a burden instead of an asset to the very King she struggled for so long to crown. Even the fact that Charles VII was adamant about her divine calling (which is not the situation) the fact was that it had become politically unpopular being associated with her. As a result, He retreated and was not serious about trying to negotiate her release or making attempts to save her. In the cruel, dog-eater physical world of princes and kings and princes, it's usually innocent people who are left to pay the ultimate cost.

It is believed that she was burnt on the spot because she was witches. However, that was not the scenario. She was tried in the English-held Rouen in an ecclesiastical tribunal for a plethora of charges. In the majority of accounts, she stood up to the accusers. It was believed that the trial was an open trial before it was shut down as well as the reasons she might have been tortured, and also why the more than 70 charges made against her were reduced to her most prominent crimes, including those relating to men's attire and her assertion that she had Godly communications.

When she was 1431 she was given life imprisonment for a signed confession to her transgressions and a promise to change her conduct. The reason she might have signed was out of fear of the penalty of being executed by burning or perhaps due to her lack of literacy and was unable to comprehend the terms she had to sign. In any case, she'd challenge it just two days later. One of the reasons is that, while in a military prison (as as opposed to the church-run prison that was more appropriate for the situation) she was feared by her male guards wearing female attire. She was in danger of being raped and tortured, which is why she returned to her previous methods of wearing male clothes. She also claimed that she heard her voice again, and they were not happy with her decision to cave her accusers.

They permitted her judges to find her guilty of being an "relapsed" heretic which brought her to the cross at the marketplace in Rouen in the month day of May 1431. She asked for the cross to be placed in front of her when she passed away and was blessedly accepted. There were rumours that thousands of people witnessed her burning and many found themselves crying and/or scared as the executioner, who was reported to be anxious at the thought of burning the saint of his day. Legend says that her heart escaped the fire.

This is just one of the many stories told about her death and the truth can be discovered somewhere between the two. The story goes that she died of smoking, but she was repeatedly burned because her organs were spared. The third attempt concluded with her ashes scattered over the Seine.

For many years there was a belief and hope that some of the remains were retrieved from the bottom of the burning pyre. The controversial relics discovered in the Paris apothecary in 1867 appeared to support this belief as well, and by the beginning of the 2000s, a group of international researchers was allowed to examine the relics. Initial findings, which were shared with the public in 2006, looked promising. A cat's femur was discovered and was similar to the customs of medieval times to throw cats of black color in the fire of witches. The cloth that was recovered from the apothecary appeared to fit with the time. The possibility of finding answers was as well sparked by the availability of technology that could identify the date of birth and regional origins of the cloth and what the specific gender was of the body and the death date of the deceased and how often the body was burned during an extended period. These, according to scientists will help distinguish and distinguish Joan of Arc from other people who were executed in the same manner. In 2007, however the remains found in 1867 were not to be the saint's. They appeared to be of an Egyptian mummified mummy and the remains of a powdered mummy that were used to treat ailments in the past. The bones that were mummified date back to about the 7th to the middle of the 3rd Century B.C., with the cat bone dating back to the same period and being mummified. The DNA was not able to be extracted from the specimen. Whatever the location where the rest of Joan of Arc ended up there, it wasn't found in any human hand.

Following the death of her mother, the bloody conflict she had helped continue for another two decades. However, her brief participation was like the metaphorical tossing of a pebble, which caused ripples and wide-ranging results.

The first was that The English loss at Orleans demonstrated that they were not invincible , and that their victory was not a certainty. It might or may not have played a role in decisions such as that made by Philip the Good and his decision to change sides could be a devastating loss to English goals. Philip the Good is believed to have recognized that the English required native collaborations in order to accomplish their ambitions for France and, by 1435, he decided that he would not let them have it. He recognized Charles VII. In 1436 Paris had come under authority by Charles VII, the French King. There were other victories for France (especially when England involved within the Wars of the Roses, that were largely due to their flimsy efforts in France in the beginning) until, eventually, England had only Calais (which was later surrendered).

The French prevailed the battle and Charles VII kept his crown. The king and other prominent voices ultimately fought for a retrial for Joan who was removed of charges by Pope Calilixtus III during the year 1450s. Joan was declared to be a martyr. Although this might seem like an opportunity to allow Charles VII to right a wrong however, it is believed it was motivated by political reasons to investigate Joan's innocence, because the conviction of her discredits her, her verdict was a way to give the successful French King more credibility.

THE ICON
The process of being declared a saint is the final stage of an extensive, complex procedure. There is a waiting period to determine if the person who is being evaluated has a lasting impact that stands the tests of time. Petitions are submitted at different levels within the Church, and the subsequent review and collection of documents could take

several years. Votes are cast when the case for sainthood is made up the ladder of approval prior to and after the necessary number of miracles that have to be exclusively attributed to the saint who is being sought out, that must be documented with care and scrutiny to determine if the miracle can be caused through natural causes or any other intercessors.

It's a long and intricate procedure that is more complex for saints than for others. Joan of Arc had to wait until after 500 years her death before she was recognized as a saint in the Roman Catholic Church in May 16th, 1920.

In the present, more than 100 years later than that centuries-long wait for her canonization she remains an object of speculation. Based on the beliefs you believe in one can feel content in the knowledge in the belief that Joan of Arc was indeed an authentic messenger from God and that she heard saintly voices, and that these were the factors which allowed her to achieve all the incredible things she accomplished. Many saintly stories end this way. However, given the amount of documents available about her life and telling of a compelling story and with a character so strong that many could not resist digging into the possibilities.

"The ambitious" Genius. In the context of an individualistic view there is a possibility that she was simply an ambitious genius who embraced the concept of "voices" to ensure that she could be heard in a hierarchical, male-dominated society, with the motive being that she was looking for ways to increase her standing. The opportunistic streak wasn't in the family of her in any case. At one point the brothers of her are said to have received meals and gifts, while presenting an untrue sister for years following her execution. was executed.

A sick girl. For those who would prefer reasoning from the medical profession

There are a myriad of theories regarding the reason for Joan of Arc's plight that she was hearing voices as she may be suffering from schizophrenia (a disorder with multiple personality) epilepsy, schizophrenia or another condition that causes hallucinations and illusions, such as bipolar disorder, migraine or brain injuries. A "cowgirl," as she was referred to by her English adversaries, might be infected with bovine tuberculosis caused by unpasteurized milk or her contact with the animals she kept. There was something not quite charming about her erratic temper and she was not scared to take on physical punishment. Slapping the enemies of war, she may not have been able to do, however there are reports where she's raised her arms against her enemies in the event of an act she considered offensive.

A Sexual Subversive. If you were to look at her through a gender-specific lens or perhaps, she may have been transgressing the norms of sexuality by moving to divorce, dressing as males, actively participating in the wars and, as has been reported in certain circles she had relationships to other females (she did dress in men's clothing and spent a significant amount of time with a group of other women at night, however, her devoted followers claim that her clothing was worn to be able to blend in with soldiers and to make her appear more seriously, whereas evening female friendship was an old-fashioned way for married women to join together to provide warmth and security particularly in camps that were dominated by males). Propaganda Figure. Through a political lens some experts say Joan of Arc as she was referred to was more of a fabricated character than a real woman an earnest , religious visionary or mad country girl maybe who was able to chew too much than she was able to bite when she became involved in wartime politics and was then molded by the forces of the day to become a mythology that which they could utilize to gain advantage. After she had outlived her value her time, she was then put to rest.

In some ways , this was the case. Symbolism was and remains so vital in the world of politics. It was her role to be a beacon of optimism, a rallying point for a flagging cause. Why should a king who is savvy make use of her to achieve his own purposes? She was groomed and adorned at least from the time she entered the realm of the politically adept, Yolande from Aragorn. As she was geared for battle with guns and an army and her image was nurtured and worked for a while. She encouraged enlistments, energized soldiers who were demoralized, and pushed exhausted soldiers in the field. She instilled fear and fear among her foes. It is not difficult to see her presence on the battlefield and her name and the appearance of her distinctive flag... have brought victory many times for France. While she was celebrated during victory, the fame diminished after a bitter tasting of defeat as did those who fought for her. Even after her death her canonization might have proved to be a useful political tool in the era of the time; the French were fighting and hoping to unite her troops, while they were hoping to rally their troops, and the Holy See is fighting the atheists and communism, having a symbol of the Catholic faith in Joan.

What she did However, it shouldn't negate her work or her claim to have a divine purpose. Both are inextricably linked; she could have been a genuine visionary, but she was also employed by people who were around her (and following her) to further their own purposes simultaneously. The issue is how to separate facts from fiction. What percentage of the actions believed to be hers actually occurred? Are the proofs for her prophecies only influenced through the lens of hindsight? Could some stories concerning her made up? There's no conclusive answer to thesequestions, regardless of the numerous documents that are written about her life. Even the accounts of contemporary times were contradictory and contradictory, which is unusual due to the chaos of the war. What is confirmed and is widely confirmed is definitely an act of courage (and possibly holy) enough. She was an ordinary girl who achieved a remarkable number of things, even though she started from scratch. She strove to create the world to conform to her idea that was the right thing to do. She preached piety, devotion and devotion to God and led by the example of her parents. She was a martyr for her country. She was burned to death for her beliefs.

The influence of her iconography and image is such that , long after her death Joan of Arc continued to be used to promote political goals. The image was utilized to inspire Frenchmen during the Franco-Prussian War from 1870-1871. Her image was utilized by anti-Semites, nationalists and political figures of the far right during the 1900s. Her image was an effective symbol of the Allied forces during World Wars I and II and was a vilifier of her fellow Germans (especially during the time that bombs destroyed the Cathedral in Reims). In France her image resonated due to German aggression in the area where she was born as well as for Americans and for the British the image of her was utilized to inspire women to join in the war by purchasing bonds. Through her later years her image became extremely powerful and adaptable, so that it was able to appeal to nearly everyone. The monarchists who fought for their cause as well as those who are a believer in self-determination meritocracy, and a republic; all spectrums of opinion from the left to the right In every war or conflict that the French encountered themselves, specifically for women, and for women, and for the LGBTQ community.

With all the positive and negative aspects her growth has gone beyond her initial goals. It's almost talisman (though she wouldn't want it to be because of her devotional nature) the way her image is re-created every time for various reasons. It is only a matter of time before the eternal, powerful image of this saintly woman is utilized with care, and with the same compassion and mercy she showed even to her enemies, towards the betterment of humanity.

Chapter 11: Childhood

1. Joan of Arc was born in 1412 in the town of Domremy in the northeastern region of France. The daughter was Jacques d'Arc and his wife Isabelle and she had three brothers older than her three brothers - Jacquemin, Jean, and Pierre and a younger sister named Catherine.

The place where Joan was born is Domremy

2. Joan was raised by a rural family with a low income and was a part of the caretaker team for the animals of the farm. Like many of the kids in her village she was not a student at school and didn't learn to write or read.

Joan watching her sheep

3. The d'Arc family was extremely religious. Isabelle taught her daughter an ardent love for the doctrines from the Catholic Church. Joan regularly attended mass and attended church with her parents on every Sunday.

4. When she was 13 years older, Joan was in her father's garden when she heard voices talking to her. She looked up to see the direction that the voice came from and noticed an intense light that she believed was Saint Michael The angel who is the leader of God's army.
Joan hearing her voices

5. As time passed over time, Saint Michael got to be joined by two angels saints - Saint Margaret and Saint Catherine and Saint Catherine. They urged Joan to become a responsible girl, to obey her parents and to attend the church.

6. Joan continued to receive frequent visits from the angels but at the age of sixteen years old, they delivered the angels with a brand new message. She had to be the hero of France by leading an army that would defeat the English and ensure that an French monarch could again be crowned the throne of France.

7. Joan was shocked at what angels advised that she must do. She was a mere peasant girl without any army training. How would she lead an army in the midst of the power of English? However, her deep faith assured the girl that with God's guidance any thing was feasible.

8. The next heir to the throne in France would be Charles, who was the son of the previous French monarch, and he was often referred to for his nickname, the "Dauphin." Court of the Dauphin was in Chinon, a town in Chinon situated 350 miles (560 kilometers) away from Domremy. Contrary to the wishes of her parents, Joan decided to go there to convince the Dauphin to place her in the command of an army to eliminate out the English away from France in order for him to become the king.

Charles the Dauphin

Leave Home

9. The way to Chinon will be via English territory The journey would be through English territory, and Joan required assistance in getting there in a safe manner. Joan decided to visit the town nearby of Vaucouleurs where there was an army of French soldiers, and ask for an escort to the treacherous journey.

10. As she arrived at Vaucouleurs, Joan went to meet the garrison commander, Robert de Beaudricourt. She told him about her visits from angels in order to help save France and to put the Dauphin on the throne. However, Beaudricourt laughed at her and instructed her to go home.

11. However, Joan did not give up and continued to Vaucouleurs in Vaucouleurs, where word spread among those in the community about that girl for a mission to help save France. Beaudricourt was informed the growing amount of those who believe Joan was being sent on a mission by God and then decided to visit her again. He was aware

about the prediction that said a woman could be the savior for France Maybe Joan was the maid?

12. When Beaudricourt saw Joan once more, he was awestruck by her determination . He wrote an email for the Dauphin to request a visit. After the Dauphin was willing, Beaudricourt handed Joan an escort from soldiers to take her on the long journey to Chinon.

13. The trip to Chinon could be risky for a young lady So Joan cut off her hair and disguised herself as a male. In February 1429 Joan and her escort quit Vaucouleurs on horseback and were greeted in the direction of the town's inhabitants. They arrived at Chinon 11 days afterward.

A meeting with the Dauphin

14. Though the Dauphin was aware of Joan through the letter of Beaudricourt however, he was not sure if she was telling the truth about voices coming from God as well as angels. He decided

to put the girl up for a test by cloning his appearance in plain clothing.

15. When Joan was at the castle of Dauphin and was shown into a room brimming with knights and courtiers. Only one person who was wearing the dress of the Dauphin and the voices in Joan's head advised her to not look at the man and look for the sole person in plain clothes. When she finally found the person she knelt in front of him, saying, "You are the Dauphin."

16. The Dauphin believed of the fact that Joan was the one who would be the one to save France and he listened intently to the plans she had. With the blessing of God she would be the leader of the Dauphin's Army , and take all the English from France before setting her Dauphin to the French throne.

17. The Dauphin was amazed by Joan and presented her with an armored suit that was specially designed as well as a beautiful white horse, as well as an

emblem to wear to combat. However, Joan declined the blade to the Dauphin.

18. Joan's voices had informed her about a sword that was hidden in the chapel nearby. A servant was dispatched to find it which led to the discovery of the weapon. located exactly in the spot Joan was claiming it was. The sword was covered in corrosion, which dissolved when it was pulled up to reveal a stunning sparkling sword.

Joan dressed in her armor and sporting a banner and sword

19. When Joan was a part of her Army as a soldier, she demanded her soldiers behave politely and use no foul language, and attend the church. Some soldiers were not happy about receiving orders from an unmarried woman, and there was plenty of wrangling but they were also inspired by Joan and soon began to admire her. Joan as well as her Army were now prepared to fight.

Victory at Orleans

20. Joan's first encounters with the English would take place in her home city, Orleans 100 miles (160 kilometers) north-east of Chinon and at the frontier of the enemy's territory. Orleans was under English besieged for six months, and there was no food and no supplies being brought to the town. People were struggling to eat and were on the verge of abandoning the city.

21. The English had constructed strongholds in the ring around Orleans to prevent anyone from who wanted to leave or enter the city. However, there was an unguarded gate, not secured within the city wall which allowed Joan and a few members of her troops to access Orleans without a trace, carrying much-needed food and other supplies.

15th-century Orleans

22. To get to Orleans, Joan would first be required to traverse the Loire which is the river along which the city sits. The only option to traverse the river was via boat, however the wind was going in the

opposite direction. Joan exclaimed, "God will help us!" - and the winds changed and she and her men could sail across the river and reach Orleans.

23. Following the crossing of the river Joan was able to ride into Orleans riding her horse. Her story was told before her, and she was welcomed by crowds of cheers that now believe that God was with them.

Joan entering Orleans

24. On the 4th of May 1429, French as well as the English Armies were reunited in the very first battle. The fight for Orleans took place for five days until the English were driven out of the city. Joan was wounded in the battle, but she refused to quit, encouraging her troops to fight more.

Joan during the battle for Orleans

25. Orleans was a huge victory that was awe-inspiring and the tale of Joan's participation in it was heard all over the world. The next step of her divine task

was to witness the Dauphin be crowned as the new King.

Coronation

26. French monarchs were typically honored in the town of Reims located just 150 miles (240 km) north from Orleans and deep within the territory of the enemy. Even though Orleans was freed from the English however, there were thousands of soldiers from the enemy occupying large areas of northern France.

27. To get to Reims, Joan and her Army had to fight battle against her enemies the English in the villages and towns which stood between them. However, town after town lost to the French after they English quit and fled to the north, with Joan's army on the move. The English were able to stop their escape at Patay, the city of Patay in the town of Patay, where they chose to stay and engage in battle against the French.

28. The Battle of Patay took place on the 18th of June 1429. It was decisive to the French. More than half of the English Army died, and the loss of only 3 French lives. Joan and her troops can now make their way to Reims in France, where the Dauphin might finally be named.

29. The Dauphin was Dauphin was crowned Charles VII of France in Reims Cathedral on July 17 in Reims Cathedral, with Joan sitting by his side. However, despite it being an event of joyous celebration, Joan felt that her job was not done. Even though the French had been able to regain a significant portion of their territory, a large portion north France was still under English control, including the capital, Paris.

Charles VII's coronation Charles VII

Defeat at Paris

30. Joan considered it essential that the capital city of France be returned back into French hands, however the new king wasn't as certain. King Charles did not

like conflict and wanted to negotiate arrangements with English So he refused Joan permission to launch an attack on Paris.

31. Instead of fighting the English yet again The King Charles signed an arrangement to the Duke of Burgundy that was fighting behalf in the battle against the English. The agreement stipulated 15 days during which there would be no fighting. At the end of this period, Paris was handed over to by the French.

The Duke of Burgundy

32. However, the Duke of Burgundy was not planning on keeping his promise to the King and took advantage of this time to strengthen the strength of his Army to prepare an eventual French attack.

33. Joan was skeptical of her Duke Burgundy and believed that he'd lied to the King. She knew that a large number of French soldiers were ready to join her. So she put an army of soldiers and marched off to Paris.

34. The fight for Paris began at noon in the morning of September 8. After hours of battle, Joan was trying to cross the moat , which was a part of the city's walls when she was struck in the thigh with the English arrow. As she fell to the ground, wounded in the thigh, the French soldiers became discouraged and the war ended. Joan was able to shout at her troops to be careful. Paris was a possibility to have captured.

Injured in the fight for Paris

35. The next morning, Joan was eager to return to fighting, however word came from King Charles who had issued the instruction to stop the fight. All the things Joan did in her military career was success, but she was facing her first defeat.

36. Then, reluctantly, Joan returned to the court of King Charles who taken care of as her injured leg healed. The king was rewarded Joan by giving her family the noblest of noblewomen. However, Joan was not interested in being noble. All she

desired was to see France to become free from the English.

Capture and Prison

37. Joan's wound was eventually healed and then in the spring of 1430, King Charles ordered Joan to guard the Compiegne town that was under attack by Dukes of Burgundy and English soldiers.

38. On the 22nd of May, Joan arrived at Compiegne with a small number of soldiers in order to fight the vast English Army. The next day , they quit the town to confront the adversaries but Joan and her troops were soon besieged. She was taken off the horse she was riding on and later taken into custody.

A 15th-century image from the Battle of Compiegne

39. Joan was brought before the Duke of Burgundy who accepted an offer of 10,000 francs from English to surrender her to them. The English were seeking

revenge on the numerous losses which Joan suffered against them.

40. The news of Joan's abduction was announced, the population of France demanded the King Charles to offer a ransom in order to ensure Joan could be freed. However, Charles refused to pay. Charles did not agree and in November 1430 Joan was given by the English.

41. The English will put Joan in the dock for trial, accused of witchcraft as well as heresy. If they could prove Charles VII had been put in the throne through an unfaithful witch, he would be discredited which would make it much easier for an English King to assume the reigns of France.

42. The English transported Joan into the city of Rouen in France, where she was put for trial. The trial lasted for two months. prison, and was chained and guarded every day and at night with English soldiers. On the 21st of February 1431 she was brought to Rouen Castle, where her trial was scheduled to begin.

Everything that is left of the 13th-century Rouen Castle

On Trial

43. Joan was forced to sit on a tiny stool before a plethora of judges who were slated to judge her. They all swore at her and wanted her declared guilty. Joan was without a defense her and she had to be reliant on her quick-witted wits to respond to the numerous questions from the opposition that could be posed to her in the course of trial.

44. The trial ran for many weeks, and despite the fact that Joan was a nineteen year old farm girl who was unable to write or read but she was able to give a convincing story of her life as interrogators attempted to catch her. However, day after day of constant questions ended up leaving Joan exhausted and confused and she frequently said things she wasn't intending to say.

45. At the conclusion of her trial Joan was taken to a burial ground where there was a wooden stakes used to torch people to death. It was said that if she confessed her guilt , she could avoid being burned alive.

46. Frightened and exhausted, Joan lost her nerve for the first time. She confessed to the police the voice she was hearing were not real. She was also able to say that she would no longer wear the clothes of men (which she was doing throughout the course of her career in military) and not to participate in war. This prevented Joan from being burned to death however she was instead sentenced to life in prison.

47. Joan quickly regained her confidence and was remorseful about making the vow. She claimed that she'd committed the act because she was afraid and the voices that were in her head were really coming from God. When she retracted her confession, Joan was convicted of burning to death.

Death & Sainthood

48. Around 8 o'clock on day of 30th, 1431 Joan was taken to the market in Rouen and an estimated 10,000 people assembled to watch her die. Joan wore a dress that was coated with sulphur to prevent it from burning easily. She also wore a pointed hat that had listed a list on her "crimes."

49. Joan was shackled to a sturdy, wooden stake, and demanded an altar to stand on it, which was handed to her by an obedient English soldier. She humbly repaid her accusers, before an open flame was lit around her. When the smoke and flames consumed herbody, the crowd could hear her voice, "Jesus, Jesus, Jesus ...."

Joan was tied to the stake

50. The conflict between France and England was fought for another twenty years following Joan's death until the English returned to their homeland and France was again at peace.

51. After the war ended, Charles VII ordered an investigation into the trial. It did not find Joan guilty of any felony. A little over 500 years later at the age of 20, she was declared an saint from the Roman Catholic Church and is currently a patron saint for France.

A variety of Joan of Arc Facts
52. While Joan of Arc owned a sword, she wasn't one to make use of it during battle because she didn't want to hurt anyone. In lieu of the sword Joan carried her flag, and inspired the soldiers around her to be courageous.

53. The time Charles VII made Joan and her family noblewomen and noblemen He gave Joan an armorial badge with two fleur-de lys (lilies that represent France) as well as an eagle holding an emerald crown. The awarding of the coat of arms demonstrates the importance Joan was a symbol to Charles VII. Charles.
Joan of Arc's coat of arms

54. In 1415 in 1415, at the time that Joan of Arc was three years old in 1415, Joan of Arc was just three years old. French were defeated in a humiliating manner at Agincourt which saw the 7,000 English soldiers defeated the 20000-strong French Army. 14 years later, the French took revenge in The Battle of Patay was as embarrassing on those English as Agincourt was for the French and the 55,000-strong English army was defeated only 1500 French soldiers.

55. Joan of Arc is a national hero in France as well as there's statues dedicated to her across France, and even in Orleans which was the city she repelled the English from in 1429. There are also sculptures depicting Saint Joan across other countries, like those in the United States. The statue of Joan of Arc was unveiled in 1972 in New Orleans, Louisiana - an offer from the French people to celebrate New Orleans' French heritage.

Conclusion

Joan of Arc is one of the few historical characters of Europe. Her impact on the world was profound. Joan's ability to inspire and improve morale of French who had been shut down for many years under the English bosses was impressive. In England, Joan of Arc was given a high status. A formal reconciliation ceremony took place in the cathedral of Winchester.

Joan of Arc was the supreme patriot. Her love for France was deeply rooted within her heart and mind. However, for the last 23 years the king Charles VI tried to conceal the fact that she played a major part in the acquisition of the entirety of his beloved nation of France. In a bid to stop that for long, he was able to declare her name. Everyone who struggled with her felt a connection with her soul. After she had escaped the confines of death, they felt her with their hearts. This was a significant moment for them. In contrast to the King and others, they did not abandon her. The Church discovered a fresh saint within the form of a woman with no impressive military record but adept at feats which only come from invisibly and mysterious forces beyond the realm of mortals.

www.ingramcontent.com/pod-product-compliance
Lightning Source LLC
Chambersburg PA
CBHW050404120526
44590CB00015B/1825